CROSS-CULTURAL ESSENTIALS 5

LANGUAGE AND LINGUISTICS

A COMPREHENSIVE LOOK AT THE NATURE, STRUCTURE AND VARIATION OF LANGUAGE

TUTORIALS WITH DISCUSSION
INTS AND ACTIVITIES

Language and Linguistics
A Comprehensive look at the nature, structure and variation of language
Communication Foundations, Module 5 of the Cross-Cultural Essentials Curriculum

Copyright © 2019 AccessTruth

Version 1.1

ISBN: 978-0-6484151-3-8

All Rights Reserved. Except as may be permitted by the Copyright Act, no part of this publication may be reproduced in any form or by any means without prior permission from the publisher. Requests for permission should be made to info@accesstruth.com

Unless otherwise indicated, all Scripture quotations are taken from the Holy Bible, New Living Translation, copyright © 1996, 2004. Used by permission of Tyndale House Publishers, Inc., Wheaton, Illinois 60189. All rights reserved.

Published by AccessTruth
PO Box 8087
Baulkham Hills NSW 2153
Australia

Email: info@accesstruth.com
Web: accesstruth.com

Cover and interior design by Matthew Hillier
Edited by Simon Glover

Table of Contents

About the Cross-Cultural Essentials Curriculum 5

TUTORIAL 5.1 7
Basic Concepts

TUTORIAL 5.2 13
Basic Concepts - Introduction to Linguistics

TUTORIAL 5.3 21
Phonetics 1

TUTORIAL 5.4 27
Phonetics 2

TUTORIAL 5.5 37
Phonetics 3

TUTORIAL 5.6 47
Phonetics 4

TUTORIAL 5.7 55
Phonetics 5

TUTORIAL 5.8 63
Phonology 1

TUTORIAL 5.9 71
Phonology 2

TUTORIAL 5.10 83
Morphology 1

TUTORIAL 5.11 93
Morphology 2

TUTORIAL 5.12 101
Syntax 1

TUTORIAL 5.13 117
Syntax 2

TUTORIAL 5.14 135
Language and Meaning

TUTORIAL 5.15 139
Semantics 1

TUTORIAL 5.16 153
Semantics 2

TUTORIAL 5.17 163
Pragmatics

TUTORIAL 5.18 175
Language and Identity

TUTORIAL 5.19 185
Language and Dialects

TUTORIAL 5.20 195
Language Families

TUTORIAL 5.21 205
Language Change

TUTORIAL 5.22 213
Language Types and Variation

About the Cross-Cultural Essentials Curriculum

It's no secret that there are still millions of people in the world living in "unreached" or "least-reached" areas. If you look at the maps, the stats, and the lists of people group names, it's almost overwhelming. The people represented by those numbers can't find out about God, or who Jesus Christ is, or what He did for them because there's no Bible in their language or church in their area – they have *no access* to Truth.

So you could pack a suitcase and jump on a plane, but then what? How would you spend your first day? How would you start learning language? When would you tell them about Jesus? Where would you start? The truth is that a mature, grounded fellowship of God's children doesn't just "happen" in an unreached area or even in your neighbourhood. When we speak the Truth, we need to have the confidence that it is still the same Truth when it gets through our hearer's language, culture and worldview grid.

The *Cross-Cultural Essentials* curriculum, made up of 10 individual modules, forms a comprehensive training course. Its main goal is to help equip believers to be effective in providing people access to God's Truth through evangelism and discipleship. The *Cross-Cultural Essentials* curriculum makes it easy to be better equipped for teaching the whole narrative of the Bible, for learning about culture and worldview and for planting a church and seeing it grow.

More information on the curriculum can be found at *accesstruth.com*

Introduction to Module 5: Language and Linguistics

Language and Linguistics (Module 5 of the *Cross-Cultural Essentials* curriculum) equips participants in some of the more technical areas of language and linguistics. Beginning with the basic concepts, it gives introductions and practical exercises in the following areas: phonetics, phonology, morphology, syntax, language and meaning, semantics, pragmatics, language and identity, languages and dialects, language change and language families.

ABOUT THE CROSS-CULTURAL ESSENTIALS CURRICULUM

How to use this module

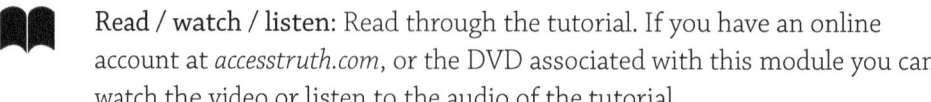

Read / watch / listen: Read through the tutorial. If you have an online account at *accesstruth.com*, or the DVD associated with this module you can watch the video or listen to the audio of the tutorial.

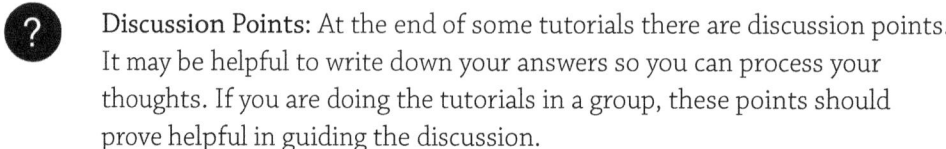

Discussion Points: At the end of some tutorials there are discussion points. It may be helpful to write down your answers so you can process your thoughts. If you are doing the tutorials in a group, these points should prove helpful in guiding the discussion.

Activities: Some tutorials have activities that involve practical tasks, worksheets that need to be completed, or may just ask for a written answer.

Primary Contributors

Paul and Linda Mac

Paul Mac and his wife, Linda, spent 11 years in Papua New Guinea involved in pioneering church planting in an isolated people group. They were privileged to see God plant a number of churches in that area that continue to thrive today. During the time there, they headed up a translation team that produced a New Testament in the local language. After leaving PNG, Paul and Linda worked for 12 years in leadership and consultative roles with an international mission agency. Today they continue to provide church planting guidance for a number of different teams engaged in some of the world's most challenging contexts. They are passionate about seeing churches planted that are well equipped to carry on for future generations.

5.1 Basic Concepts

OBJECTIVES OF THIS TUTORIAL

This tutorial introduces the basic concepts of linguistics. It will give brief answers to the questions: 'What is linguistics?', 'What is language?' and 'What is grammar?'

Introduction

Before we begin to focus in on the details - let's look back and remember how the concept of language fits into God's story. Our Creator is also the creator of language, and His authority and power over that fundamental area of human existence were clearly demonstrated in a dramatic event in the history of the world.

Remember God's account of a time more than three generations after the Great Flood, when a civilization had settled in a plain of Babylonia. (Genesis 11:1-4) These people's great-grandparents had been eyewitnesses of the global destruction of the flood and had been in the boat God had used to preserve them and the animals - but already they had moved far away from an appropriate appreciation of Him as Creator. They had given up coming to Him in the way He had graciously given to humans after the fall – in faith, with the sacrifice of animals. They were arrogantly telling their own story and in their blind ambition, made a concerted effort to build a great tower for all to see. It was to reach to the sky - a monument to them - a means of physical protection and a way of preserving their reputation for generations to come. The name of the tower of course, is Babel.

God was unwilling to let them gather their strength and resources together in a concerted denial of their need for Him, their Creator. (Genesis 11:5-9) He graciously gave them the opportunity to see their foolishness, and did something to the post-flood civilization that made it impossible for them to tell their story to each other as a homogenous group. His Narrative simply says that He *confused their languages* and that this had the effect of scattering them over the world. By doing this, God effectively stopped their rebellious intentions and also forced the fulfillment of his original intention for man, which was to populate the earth. God used something He'd gifted man with in the first place but which was now taken for granted – speech, the ability to communicate tangible facts as well as ideas and abstract concepts.

BASIC CONCEPTS

As we look into the fascinating area of language throughout the next tutorials - in its wonderful complexity and intricacy - we can also acknowledge God's amazing creative power as we investigate this gift He gave to man. We can remember that it makes sense - knowing the origin of all the world's languages - that they are amazingly complex in structure and exhibit an incredible variety, but also share many similar characteristics in spite of their variety, which point to their common origin.

In this tutorial we will be introducing some of the basic concepts in the area of *linguistics*, and in later tutorials we will be going on to look at some of those concepts in more detail. We are not setting out to study linguistics for its own sake - but because gaining a foundational understanding of *how language works* will help us to eventually become better communicators in a new context, in another language.

What is linguistics?

Linguistics is the scientific study of language. It is about trying to explain the properties of language - not individual languages - but of *language* in general. Linguistics seeks to answer questions such as:

- What is language?
- How does language work?
- What special properties does language have?
- How is language structured?
- How do children acquire their native language?
- How do people use language?

What is language?

All humans are born with an innate capacity for language - we were created that way. Language is something we do with our minds. It is a set of principles and building blocks we have stored in our minds.

Language *isn't* writing, and it *isn't* speech - not all human vocal sounds are language, and not all language uses sounds (sign languages are real languages too). So what is language? We can understand more clearly what language *is* by thinking about symbols and signs.

Iconic signs and arbitrary symbols

A *sign* is something that stands for or refers to something else. Some signs have a real relationship with the thing they refer to. They are *iconic*. They are not the thing, but they are an attempt to actually represent the thing.

A *symbol* is arbitrary – there is no relationship at all between the symbol and the thing it refers to, except that we agree that it will refer to that thing.

Look at the picture of the policeman with his stop sign. The picture of the policeman is an *iconic sign*. It is not actually a policeman (it's just pixels on your screen or ink on your paper), but it is an attempt to represent a policeman. The red shape he is holding up is a *symbol* – it means "STOP", but there is nothing about that red shape that really represents the act of stopping. We just agree this is what that particular geometric shape with a red color *means*.

It's the same in language. The group of sounds we write as *shoes* has no real relationship with the things we put on our feet. It's just a group of sounds we make with our mouths. But as speakers of English, we all agree to use that group of sounds to refer to the things we wear on our feet.

Language is a system of symbols. The relationship between meaning and linguistic form - the words used to convey meaning - is arbitrary, just like the red stop sign. The meaning of each symbol is a convention, or agreement, between speakers.

We all agree that the group of sounds we write as *cat* refers to the small furry animal. We could all agree that *cat* means something else instead, and that a different group of sounds mean the furry animal - but we would all have to agree.

This symbolic representation of meaning is a characteristic of language - not just of English, but of any language. Almost all words and all grammatical structures in all languages are arbitrary symbols that convey meaning.

There are a few examples of iconic signs in languages also - they attempt to represent the real thing - but these are the exception. Languages can have words that use onomatopoeia or sound symbolism (*bang, murmur, mumble* and *mutter*) where the actual words sound like the thing they are representing. Or, languages can use features like lengthening or repetition in an iconic way (*I waited for a loooong time* or *It happened many many many many times.*) But although true signs like these do occur in languages, they are a very insignificant part of any language – almost all words and almost all grammatical structures in any language are not iconic, but instead are arbitrary symbols. This is a defining characteristic of language.

System of rules

So, language is simply a system of symbols that represent different meanings. But it is an incredibly complex system of symbols that is only manageable because rules govern its use. In most languages, the rule systems themselves are so complex they are still not properly understood. Native speakers learn and use those rules because God gave them an inherent ability to learn and use language, not because they investigated and memorized the rules of their language.

When we say "rules" in linguistics, we don't mean something we are told to do (like "don't split infinitives" or "don't end a sentence in a preposition"). We really mean *principles* that we have stored in our minds about how to use this system of symbols. Knowledge of these rule systems is unconscious – we are not aware of it and don't have to think about it. As native speakers of our language we have this 'unconscious knowledge' or *linguistic competence* - an underlying knowledge of the language that gives us the ability to produce it.

Our actual use of language - what comes out of our mouths - often contains many and various mistakes; stammers, slips of the tongue and false starts when we lose our train of thought and have to start a sentence over again. These don't reflect our actual knowledge of the language; they reflect the influence of outside factors such as sleepiness, drink, distractions, memory lapses, etc.

But it is the underlying knowledge of language that we are interested in - the native speaker's working knowledge of the system of rules that gives him the ability to produce the right symbol at the right time to communicate clearly.

Finite rules - infinite output

All languages use the same kinds of "building blocks" (such as words) and all languages organize these building blocks into grammatical structures that help listeners to understand the meaning. These grammatical structures are built up according to very strict rules.

One of the most important universal properties of language is that it is *creative*. This means that a native speaker of a language can construct and understand *novel utterances*, utterances they've never encountered or produced before.

All languages are *finite systems* - there's a limited set of rules in any language. But every language allows for the production of an *infinite set of utterances* - there are an unlimited number of different sentences that you can make using those rules. As long as you "know the rules" of a language, you can create new grammatical sentences in that language. This is called *rule-governed creativity*.

I can say:

- *John walked home.*
- *John walked home and Bill caught the bus.*
- *John walked home and Bill caught the bus and Fred took a taxi.*
- *etc.*

Or:
- *John is tired.*
- *You know that John is tired.*
- *Tom said that you know that John is tired.*
- *I think Tom said that you know that John is tired.*
- *etc.*

I could keep on adding bits to these sentences, because there's nothing in the grammatical system that stops me from creating an infinitely long sentence. The limit is only to do with the processing power of my brain. The important point is that there is no "longest sentence" in English, or in any language. Given any sentence, however long, I can make it longer by adding *and...* or *did you know that...*

It's impossible to make a list of all the sentences of English (or of any other language). In our minds we have a *lexicon* of our language. This is a kind of word dictionary. You can't construct a "sentence dictionary" like a word dictionary, because there's not a finite set of sentences. This is true of all languages because all languages allow for the production of complex sentence patterns.

So, language is characterized by rule-governed creativity. Your knowledge of the rules of a language (your linguistic competence) makes it possible for you to produce an unlimited number of new grammatical sentences in that language. Just like a chef, who, with their knowledge of the 'rules' of how the different ingredients go together and how they should be cooked, can creatively come up with an incredible number of possible dishes.

What is grammar?

Grammar is the unconscious knowledge of the rules of a language. What we referred to earlier as *linguistic competence* is actually grammar - how the mind processes and stores language.

But... the word 'grammar' is also used to refer to our *representations* of that unconscious knowledge of the rules - a human attempt to try to simplify and describe an incredibly complex thing that God created. So, there are different kinds of 'grammars' that you may hear about: prescriptive grammar, pedagogical (i.e. teaching) grammar, descriptive grammar, generative grammar, universal grammar. All these are just *representations*, or ways to talk about and describe the rules, not actually the rules being manifested in real life.

Grammar is how the mind processes and stores language. Grammar is also a representation of how the mind processes and stores language.

BASIC CONCEPTS

Domains of grammar

So, grammar is a set of mental principles or rules, and also a description of those rules. Within the bigger set of rules we call grammar, there are different areas that use different *kinds* of rules - depending on the basic building blocks used to build different kinds of bigger structures. These are called *domains* or *levels* of grammar:

- *Phonetics* - speech sounds
- *Phonology* - organization of sounds
- *Morphology* - structure of words
- *Syntax* - structure of sentences
- *Semantics* - meaning (of words and sentences)

We will look at each of these domains in more detail throughout this module.

 DISCUSSION POINTS

1. As you think about some of the basic characteristics of language, what specific things do you see that point to a Creator, or reveal something of the character of God?

2. Do you think that it is legitimate to 'study' language in a scientific way? Why or why not?

 ACTIVITIES

1. Look at each of the six signs below. For each sign, note the following;
- Whether you think the sign is iconic or symbolic - or if it has elements of both.
- Which particular elements are symbolic, and what do you think the symbols mean?
- How did you work out, or how do you know, what the symbols mean?

5.2 Basic Concepts - Introduction to Linguistics

OBJECTIVES OF THIS TUTORIAL

This tutorial continues to explore what language is, by looking at some of the universal design characteristics of language and also how we learn language.

Introduction

In the last tutorial we said that language is an in-born human thinking ability - a mental system - something that we were created with the ability to do. We also said that language involves communicating using arbitrary symbols.

A language consists of:
- *grammar*, which is a finite set of principles speakers use to combine the building blocks of their language, and
- a *lexicon*, which is the set of words and other meaningful forms that speakers know, like a mental dictionary that they use.

We also said that language is characterized by *rule-governed creativity* – the finite set of rules that allows us to combine the finite number of forms in the lexicon to generate or create an infinite number of utterances.

We also said that linguistic competence is the unconscious knowledge of grammatical principles or rules that we have as native speakers of our language. It is the mental system we have that generates our actual linguistic performance, which in real life can be flawed with speech errors, slips of the tongue, or other mistakes.

Language as a mental system

God created people to use language - it isn't simply an *activity* that we learn to do - language is a mental system that we are born with; that He put there.

When we think about the complexities of the language system it's quite amazing that we can speak fluently, without many mistakes, with no thought about how we are speaking, or how we are constructing our sentences. How is it that we are able to do this? What is it that people do when they use language, and how is it that they can do it?

Language is learnt only partly by imitation - a child is born with the ability to learn language. The actual words of a particular language, and the possible structures that it uses, are learnt from the language around the child, but only on the basis of certain properties and principles of language that are innate - that are already in place in the mind of the child.

How are children able to learn something so complex when they are so young with no conscious learning if there is no innate ability to do so? Children can't learn language by memorizing sentences (because there is an almost infinite number of sentences in any language). They don't seem to learn language by imitation alone because:

- all children make the same kinds of systematic and consistent mistakes using forms they've never heard and so can't be imitating. (For example, over-applying rules: *runned, goed, sheeps, mans*, etc.)
- children treat complex forms as single words in contexts they have never heard them. (For example, *I want the other-one spoon*.)
- research has shown that children get reinforcement on the basis of truth conditions, not grammatical structure. When they say something factually wrong but grammatically right they are corrected (negative reinforcement). (Child: *mummy went to work yesterday* mother: *no darling, I didn't go to work yesterday*). When they say something factually right but grammatically incorrect they are not corrected (and might get positive reinforcement). (Child: *mummy goed to work yesterday* mother: *that's right darling, I did, didn't I?*).

Heart language

Linguists have noted that the ability to use language develops naturally as children get older, and that it develops following the same developmental stages in children everywhere. By the time a certain age is reached, children are able to use most of the complex structures of their language (whatever language that is, and whatever kinds of structures that language has).

Because of that, linguists think there is a period in a child's development when they acquire language naturally, and once that period is past, a person would not develop the ability to use language in the same way that children do during the period when language is normally acquired. Linguists call this a 'critical period' for language acquisition.

Learning a second language as an adult or even a teenager is different to acquiring your first language, which seems effortless. Children don't have to make a conscious effort to learn their first language, and they don't have to be taught it. It's one of the ways children naturally develop. Adults (and even teenagers) trying to learn a second language have to make much more of a conscious effort to do so - it is more a process of learning, rather than just developing naturally.

One way to look at this first language (heart language) experience is through the eyes of a child as they first come into the world and try to make sense of it. They are certainly not just learning *language*, but are actually fully engaged in trying to interpret the reality that they see around them and to communicate with the people around them. They naturally seek to communicate - actu-

ally have an overwhelming *urge* to communicate; with their parents, siblings and other people. Language is a tool they need to be able to communicate with people - they hear things named or described, and then describe and name things themselves in a particular way, with words and phrases to label certain things and certain actions, or eventually to describe concepts or ideas. Their main focus is not on the language itself, but on the people and objects around them - what is *happening* and what they want to *say and do*. They use language to engage with the people and the world around them because language is both an expression of that world and their way of expressing themselves in that world.

In most cases, a child's first language (or heart language) is the one that is forever going to be an expression of that person's deepest identity - their most profound foundational experiences and thoughts - because it is the first one they heard and used to describe the world around them and it is the first medium of their expression of themselves.

Linguists have found that some of the same features of this initial learning experience - when we learned our heart language - can be applied to adult language learning programs with great effect, producing speakers with a greater depth of ability and shared understanding of the deeper meaning that the language is expressing. A focus on learning language in real-world situations and conversations, with people, in the context of relationships, with the purpose of real communication, has been found to be more effective than learning in a theoretical environment where 'language' is studied in isolation.

Language cannot be separated from the world in which it is used, from the culture and life of the people who use it. Language should never be viewed as an isolated entity, with grammar rules that can be contained in a document, or words contained in a dictionary - language is the expression of a people, and an insight into their deepest world.

Defining language

Edward Sapir, an American anthropologist-linguist defines language like this:

Language is a purely human and non-instinctive method of communicating ideas, emotions and desires by means of voluntarily produced symbols.

"Communicating" implies that language is a shared system. Language is built on a set of conventional agreements, not individual behavior - I can't just decide to give words new meanings or new pronunciations, or to redesign sentence structure however I like.

The idea that language is "purely human" means that no other species has language. People sometimes like to think that other creatures also use language. Cockatoos and parakeets do copy speech sounds ('parroting speech'), but it is not language because it is not communication and has no internal structure. But... there has been quite a lot of research on communication in animal species; dolphins, monkeys and dogs. Why isn't this language? Animals, birds and insects *do* communicate:

- Birds pass messages of various kinds to each other - alarm calls, or alerts about food sources.
- Bees communicate very precise information about sources of food - how far it is and in what direction.
- Whales and dolphins communicate with each other over long distances.
- Dogs make different sounds in different situations to communicate to other dogs and to people.

Human language is much more complex than any communication system used by animal species. But is it just a matter of degree? Is the difference between human language and animal communication systems simply one of quantity?

Animal communication and human language

It helps us to understand what language is, by comparing it to the way animals communicate. Clearly human language is vastly more *complex* than even the most sophisticated systems of animal communication, but there are other significant differences, it is not just that we communicate in a more complex way.

Bees have highly rigid systems, with no consciousness of communication and no creativity possible - their communication is simply instinctive behavior patterns in response to stimuli. How about primates? Some say the difference between humans and even the 'highest' primates is that only humans use tools (or failing that, only humans make tools). This is not true - we now know that many animal and bird species use, or even make, tools.

The same is true of systems of communication. Chimps have about three dozen different calls which they can combine in various ways. Experiments involved in teaching chimps sign language demonstrate they can use an arbitrary communication system creatively. Some say this is not language because it is *instinctive*; there is no control over use so there is no presence of intentionality. Not so. Vervet monkeys demonstrate control over use. Vervet monkeys have three warning cries - one for snakes, one for eagles, and one for leopards. People say this is not language because it is instinctive, but even Vervets won't cry warning if no other vervets are around (so control over use, and presence of intentionality). They can even 'lie' (use a warning cry when the predator is not present).

So what are the differences between the way God made us to communicate and the way He gave animals the ability to communicate? The crucial difference between primates and humans is of course that we are made in God's image - we have the ability to know and understand Him, and the ability to choose to obey him or not. We are able to communicate with Him - in fact this is one of His greatest desires for us, that we would know and communicate with Him. Of course many linguists wouldn't point to this foundational difference between animal and human communication, but they *do* note a significant distinction in the way we communicate - pointing to our unique (unique to humans) ability to combine things to form a new thing which is then treated as a single unit (called *paradigmatic* ability). This human ability applies to other areas as well as communication systems.

Chimps' tools, unlike those of even the least technologically sophisticated humans today, are not composite - made up of different parts to make something more useful - demonstrating a lack of paradigmatic ability. Chimps have 'language ability' in the sense of the controlled and creative use of a system of communication, but it is not language because it is only sequential - memorized and copied - not combined in new ways. Human language involves considerable paradigmatic behavior - making words into phrases, phrases into sentences, etc.

This is important, because even highly intelligent animals don't have a communication system that is equivalent to language, and this indicates that language is 'built-in' to humans, it's quite literally a part of being human - part of being created 'in His image'.

Design features

Since the 1950s people have talked about *design features* of language. These features point to the One who designed language and gave humans the innate ability to use it to communicate. They also clearly distinguish human, from animal communication.

Arbitrariness
Language uses arbitrary symbols - so that the meanings are not predictable from forms (the words or sentences that are used) and forms are not predictable from meanings.

Duality of Patterning
Elements in language which have no meaning on their own, combine into units which *do* have meaning. Fewer than a hundred sound units can combine to make tens of thousands of words and an infinite number of messages (*act, cat, tac*).

Discreteness
Although language basically occurs in a continuous flow and the production of a speech sound or gesture can vary each time it is used, we are always able to process language into separate (discrete) units - we can recognise words in sentences and sounds in words (*pin, bin*).

Productivity
The ability to produce (and understand) an infinite number of messages using a finite number of elements and principles for their organization.

Displacement
The ability to convey a message about things that are remote in space and/or time from where the communication of the message takes place (*My late grandmother used to live in England*).

Stimulus free
The utterance or message that will be produced can not be predicted from anything apart from the speaker of that message. We can't tell for sure what someone is going to say before they say it.

Cultural transmission
The ability to acquire language is an inherent trait, but *particular* languages are learned. The conventions of any one particular language are passed on to the younger generation through exposure to the language in use, and through active interaction in the language.

Universal properties of language

All languages share key underlying characteristics. The central focus of linguistics is the study of these *universal properties* of language - the properties that every human language shares. These include such things as the sound systems, grammatical rules, the basic building blocks of language but also the cultural and social aspects of language as well. By looking at the universal aspects of language, and also comparing how languages *differ* in these aspects, we can gain insight into how people organize their thoughts and also how they organize themselves through their use of language. We also gain insight into how languages operate within the social structures of human communities.

Over the next series of tutorials we will be investigating some of these universal properties of language in more detail, looking at the diversity that exists within each area. We will be beginning at the most fundamental level, with *phonetics* - speech sounds.

❓ DISCUSSION POINTS

1. When children are learning their first language, what are some of the things that adults around them instinctively do - in speech or behavior - to 'help'? Think of any specific behavior you have seen. Do you think it actually does help them to learn?

2. What would you say to someone who insisted that gorillas can learn to talk and communicate in real language (if you had the freedom to explain the deepest levels of that concept to them)?

➡ ACTIVITIES

1. Do a little research on sign language. What are some of the features or characteristics of sign language that might define it as a 'real' language?

BASIC CONCEPTS - INTRODUCTION TO LINGUISTICS

➡ ASSIGNMENT

To be submitted by the end of Module 5

Find an opportunity in the next couple of months, to talk with a person who speaks English, but for whom English is not their first language. Discuss with them their first language, or heart language, and during your conversation/s with them, try to find their answers to the following questions and write up your results (you may need to ask permission to record the conversation):

- What is the language that they learned as a child - their first language?
- How many languages do they speak or have some knowledge of?
- When and how did they learn English and did they consider it difficult?
- Do other close family members speak other languages?
- Do they, or their parents or relatives, still use their mother tongue in the home?
- When they meet or speak to close family members today - siblings, mother and father, grandparents, uncles and aunts - which language do they use?
- Do they still engage with any media in their first language - TV programs, books or newspapers, radio programs, movies, etc.?
- Do they ever visit their home country, and if so, do they use English there?
- In their life here, what aspects from their original culture do they still enjoy or participate in (specific foods, religious activities, social activities or events, etc.)?
- If they were to meet a person today that they had never met before, who had the same ethnic background and heart language as themselves, how would they greet that person and what would they talk/ask about?

5.3 Phonetics 1

OBJECTIVES OF THIS TUTORIAL

This is the first of a series of tutorials on the area of phonetics - speech sounds. It outlines our purpose in studying phonetics, what phonetics is, and introduces the International Phonetic Alphabet.

Introduction

Over the next five tutorials we're going to focus on *speech sounds* - the branch of linguistics that studies these is called *phonetics*. There are several branches of phonetics, including:

- *Articulatory phonetics* - the study of how speech sounds are made,
- *Acoustic phonetics* - the study of the physical properties of speech sounds (e.g. the frequency of the waves going through the air),
- *Auditory phonetics* - the study of speech sounds from the point of view of the hearer.

We'll focus on articulatory phonetics here, because it is the most foundational and the most useful for our purpose. Acoustic and auditory phonetics are important in other fields such as speech pathology.

The study of speech sounds (which are also called *phones*) was first motivated (in the late 19th century) by the need to create orthographies (writing systems) for unwritten languages and to reform spelling in existing orthographies. Because phonetics begins with the actual speech sounds of language and attempts to write them in such a way that they can be accurately reproduced, it is an essential foundation for producing an adequate alphabet or orthography. The English phonetician, Henry Sweet (1845 -1912) is credited with founding the modern science of phonetics during his own work of reforming the English alphabet. His *Handbook of Phonetics* begins:

The importance of phonetics as the indispensable foundation of all study of language - whether that study be purely theoretical, or practical as well - is now generally admitted. **(SWEET 1877)**

Our goals in studying phonetics

Phonetics is an area where it is easy to start feeling overwhelmed – by the sheer number of sounds in language that you might need to learn to write down, by the subtle differences that are difficult to hear at first, or by the unfamiliar writing system used to write those sounds.

For most of us, phonetics takes a lot of practice and repeated listening before it sinks in. The tutorials in this course will introduce the *concepts* and some *resources* to you, so you will have opportunity to practice as much as you need to. Like all practice, you'll find you learn more effectively if you do 10 minutes every day than if you try and cram in a couple of long sessions.

The object of this course is to prepare you for a real situation where you will be working with a real language (or several) - possibly one of which has not been written down before. Remember the particular language you work with will contain a *limited* number of sounds, and you will have time to learn those as you interact with speakers of that language, and to refresh yourself on the particular phonetic sounds in that language at that time. So, the goal for this course is not for you to have memorized every possible sound that can be made by a human being and to know how to write each one. So what are our goals?

By the end of these phonetics tutorials we expect that you will know that there is an IPA (International Phonetic Alphabet) character that can represent every sound in English (or in any language). We also hope that you will understand how sounds are made, and describe how particular sounds are made using a range of criteria, such as lip position and tongue height in the mouth. We will also focus on examples from Australian English, to give you a feel for phonetics in your own dialect. Also, you will have an idea of the resources that are available to help you later on.

Remember as you go through these tutorials, your goal is not to have memorized every IPA character or the description of how every sound is articulated.

Why we don't use English spelling to represent speech sounds

In order to identify different speech sounds, we need a way of referring to them - this means we need symbols for them. A set of symbols *has* been developed - called the International Phonetic Alphabet (IPA) - which we will look at in more detail later. But first, let's see why we can't simply use the letters of the English alphabet to represent speech sounds.

The main reason is that the system of symbols needed to identify speech sounds must have a *one-to-one relation* between the symbols and the sounds they represent. This means that every symbol stands for exactly one sound, and every sound is represented by exactly one symbol. Then when we see a symbol we know immediately exactly what sound it stands for, or if we hear a sound we know which symbol to use to record that sound.

You probably already have some idea that English spelling fails dismally in having a one-to-one relation to the sounds it represents, because one letter of the English alphabet can stand for different sounds in different words. Sometimes, as speakers of English, we might not even realize that we're saying completely different sounds, because they're spelled with the same letter!

For example, take the English letter <a>. The sound spelled by <a> in *fat* is different from the sound spelled by it in *father*, and both are different from the sound in a*bout*. Say the three sounds out loud one after the other ... they are completely different sounds, but are spelled using the same letter in English. So, if we just used the English letter <a> as the symbol for a sound in a foreign word, people would not know whether we meant the sound in *fat*, in *father*, or in *about* (or some other sound). This is an example in English spelling of one symbol representing many sounds.

English spelling also has another problem - one sound can be represented by several different symbols. The sound below is exactly the same sound in all these words, but is represented many different ways in English spelling:

<ea> as in *break*,

<ay> as in *bay*,

<ai> as in *bait*,

<a> with a "silent e" at the end of the word as in *bake*,

<ey> as in *they*, and

<eigh> as in *weigh*.

The problem here is that English spelling is not a correct representation of the *pronunciation* of English. By reading the spelling, you do not know how to correctly pronounce the word. There are many other examples of this weakness in English spelling:

- Sometimes two letters stand for a single sound, such as <th> and <sh>. A sequence of two symbols should stand for a sequence of two sounds.
- Not only that, but there are actually two <th> sounds: the sound beginning the word *this* is not the same as the sound beginning the word *thing* (a fact many native speakers of English might have no conscious awareness of, although they say the right sound at the right time).
- The opposite situation also occurs: where one letter of English stands for a sequence of sounds, such as the letter <x>, which often stands for a *k* sound followed by an *s* sound. One symbol should stand for a single sound, not a sequence.
- English spelling also often has "silent letters" - there is the silent <e> which occurs

PHONETICS 1

at the end of a lot of words, the <s> in *island*, the <b> in *debt* and in *lamb*, and a lot of the letters in *knight*.

Sometimes native speakers of English might even think that they do say a sound that's not part of the normal pronunciation of the word, because it's in the spelling, or if they realize they don't, they might think that they should say it. Think about the word *few* - if you listen to it you'll hear that there's a *y* sound after the *f* sound, but where is it in

the spelling? And for speakers of Australian English - say the word *car*. Did you hear the *r* sound at all? (That's because you didn't say it.)

Not surprisingly, English spelling is difficult to learn, both for native and non-native speakers, but it does follow a system. One reason for its inconsistency it is that the sounds of English have changed over time (this is true of all languages), but English spelling has not changed as much. This means that English spelling is actually quite a good representation of how English used to be pronounced a long time ago, but it's not such a good representation of how it's pronounced today.

Sounds in other languages

So, the English alphabet is not a good way to represent the sounds of English, and it's even worse for representing the sounds of many other languages. This is because English only uses a few of all the possible speech sounds that are used by languages around the world. Even languages like French, German, and Swedish use sounds that are not found in English. Most of the world's languages don't have a traditional writing system, and many of them have sounds that are not found in English. How could we represent these so that we would know what the sounds were if we used the English writing system?

Introducing the International Phonetic Alphabet (IPA)

On the website you will find a PDF of the IPA Chart. Download it and print it out so you have it available to look at, now and for the following tutorials.

Because the English spelling system is not a good way to represent the sounds of the world's languages, we use a system that is just for making an accurate on-to-one representation of the speech sounds of a language. The system we use to represent the sounds and pronunciation of English and all the world's languages is the *International Phonetic Alphabet* (usually called the IPA for short).

The IPA gives us a one-to-one relation between sounds and symbols - each symbol stands for one and only one sound (phone), and each sound is represented by one and only one symbol.

ˈkɔfi

Everyone, even if they have the same accent, pronounces sounds slightly differently (everyone has slightly different anatomy) and even the same person doesn't pronounce sounds identically all the time. These very minor differences are of no linguistic significance, and are not represented in the IPA.

We have a choice when we're writing sounds out in IPA (technically called *transcribing*) about how detailed we want to make our transcription. Sometimes we don't represent every aspect of pronunciation (especially those that are completely predictable) depending on why we're making the transcription. We can do *narrow transcription* which is more specific, and *broad transcription* which is less specific.

The IPA was created more than a century ago, and has undergone many changes over the years - the most recent version is corrected to 2005.

The IPA is the most widely used phonetic alphabet, but not everyone uses the IPA: there's another system, called the (North) American system (sometimes called the APA) and sometimes the authors of books also introduce their own symbols.

To make it clear in the examples that we will use that we're transcribing a word using IPA, rather than spelling it using the English spelling system, we will always enclose IPA symbols and transcriptions in square brackets. E.g. [i] means the IPA symbol for a specific vowel, not the letter of the English alphabet. If we are meaning the English letter, we will use angle brackets for that purpose, e.g. the English letter <i>.

Some IPA symbols look quite similar to each other, so it's very important to take care if you are writing phonetic symbols, since if you're not careful, people might think you're writing a different symbol than the one you mean. Fonts for phonetic symbols are available free from the website of the Summer Institute of Linguistics.

❓ DISCUSSION POINTS

1. Have you ever thought much about different 'accents' of English and what people are actually doing with their mouths to produce different accents?
2. How do you feel about beginning to explore phonetics (e.g., fascinating, difficult)?
3. How would you describe the general differences between Australian English and other varieties of English?

ACTIVITIES

1. Search for an interactive IPA chart online. Listen to all the different sounds. Notice how each sound is different - each symbol represents a separate sound.

2. Search for and watch a video online introducing the International Phonetic Alphabet. We have covered some of the concepts already in this tutorial, and some things will be new to you. Don't panic, we will be covering them in the next and later tutorials - but this is a good introduction to the concepts and will help to give you a framework for learning.

3. The poem below illustrates the lack of consistency in English spelling and the reason we need a phonetic alphabet. Many words with similar pronunciation in English are spelled differently (called homophones). Rewrite the poem using correct English spelling.

> Eye halve a spelling chequer
> It came with my pea sea
> It plainly marques four my revue
> Miss steaks eye kin knot sea.
>
> Eye strike a quay and type a word
> And weight four it two say
> Weather eye am wrong oar write
> It shows me strait a weigh.
>
> As soon as a mist ache is maid
> It nose bee fore two long
> And eye can put the error rite
> Its really ever wrong.
>
> Eye have run this poem threw it
> I am shore your pleased two no
> Its letter perfect in it's weigh
> My chequer tolled me sew.
>
> (Sauce unknown)

5.4 Phonetics 2

OBJECTIVES OF THIS TUTORIAL

This tutorial continues to look at the area of phonetics - speech sounds. We will take a closer look at the vocal tract to see *how* and *where* different speech sounds are physically produced, and how sounds are classified according to these factors.

Introduction

In articulatory phonetics we classify speech sounds in terms of how they're made, so to do this we need to know something about the parts of the body used in speaking. It will be very helpful to you as you learn and work with another language to understand how some of the sounds of that language are physically produced.

The Vocal Tract

Together, the parts of the body used for producing speech sounds are referred to as the **vocal tract**.

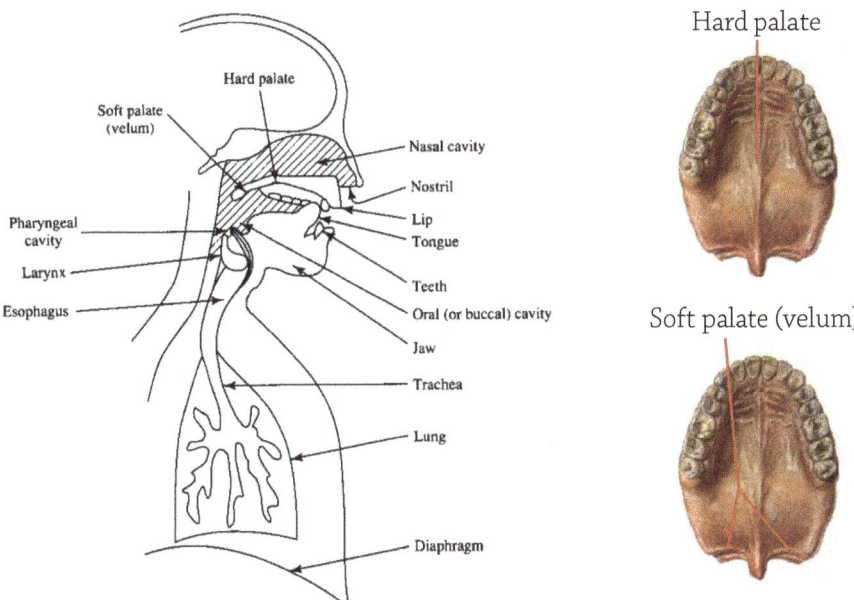

The Airstream

Most speech sounds, including all those in English, are produced with air pushed up and out from the *lungs*. The air goes up through a tube called the *trachea* (also called the windpipe) then through a box of cartilages called the *larynx*. Inside the larynx there are two muscular folds - these have traditionally been called the *vocal cords*, though in fact they're not strings, but folds, so many people refer to them as the *vocal folds*. Air then passes through the *oral cavity* (the mouth)...and sometimes through the *nasal cavity* (the nose).

Most speech sounds involve air coming out – they are *egressive*. A few sounds in some languages involve air sucked inwards – they are *ingressive*. Most speech sounds involve air coming all the way up from the lungs – they are *pulmonic*. So, most sounds in most languages are *pulmonic egressive* sounds - made when air comes up from the lungs and then comes out.

A few sounds in some languages involve air pushed in or out just from the mouth (with the larynx closed) – they are *glottalic*. Sounds with the larynx closed and air pushed out of the mouth (egressive glottalic) are *ejectives*. Sounds with the larynx closed and air sucked into the mouth (ingressive glottalic) are *implosives*. A few sounds in some languages involve air drawn into the mouth with the back of the mouth closed – they are ingressive *velaric*. These are *clicks*.

'Voiced' and 'Voiceless' sounds

The vocal folds (sometimes called the vocal cords - inside the larynx) can be positioned in a number of ways. These different positions are called *glottal states* because the *glottis* is the space between the vocal folds. Different glottal states create different kinds of sounds. For describing the sounds of Australian English and most other languages we only need to know about two of these, *voiced* and *voiceless*.

Voiced sounds involve the vocal folds being close together, but not tightly closed. Air can still flow out between them, and when it does, it makes them vibrate. This vibration is called voicing. You can feel it if you touch your throat while making the *z* sound as in *buzz*.

If, on the other hand, the vocal folds are held relatively far apart, they won't vibrate when the air passes up between them. This glottal state is called *voiceless(ness)*, and sounds involving this state are called *voiceless* sounds. An example of a voiceless sound is the *s* sound as in *bus*. If you touch your throat while making this sound you won't feel the vibration that you feel when making the *z* sound.

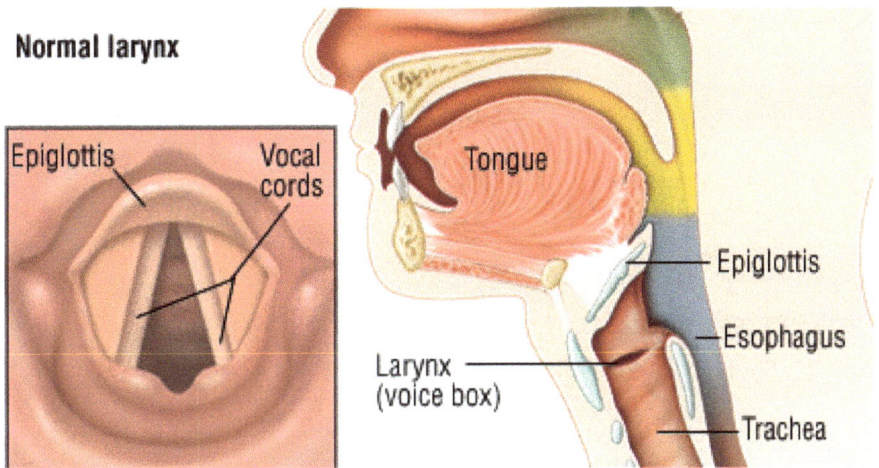

When the vocal folds are apart, as in the diagram above, a voiceless sound will result. When they are together, a voiced sound is made.

To see vocal folds in action, a quick online search will show many videos.

Consonants and vowels

A traditional way of classifying speech sounds, and one that everyone is familiar with, is the distinction between *vowels* and *consonants*. Basically the difference is that consonants involve some significant obstruction of the airflow (either complete obstruction, or enough narrowing to cause noise), while vowels don't involve a significant obstruction.

Say the following sounds (English vowel sounds) out loud - <a> <e> <i> <o> <u>. Now say the following consonants, and listen to difference - <b> <d> <f> <g> <k> <m> <z>. Did you notice the different ways in which you obstructed the flow of air (with your lips, tongue, teeth...) as you made the second set of sounds?

One group of sounds, called *glides*, is in between consonants and vowels. Glides are like vowels in articulation (the way they are said), but they pattern or function as consonants (in the way they are used). For this reason glides are usually put with the consonants in tables - in the standard IPA chart, there's no separate row for glides - they're placed among the *approximants* (this term will be explained soon).

Consonants

As well as glottal state (voiced or voiceless), consonants are classified by two factors: one is which vocal organs are used to obstruct the flow of air - we call this the *place of articulation*. The other is how much obstruction there is, and what kind of obstruction it is - we call this the *manner of articulation*.

PHONETICS 2

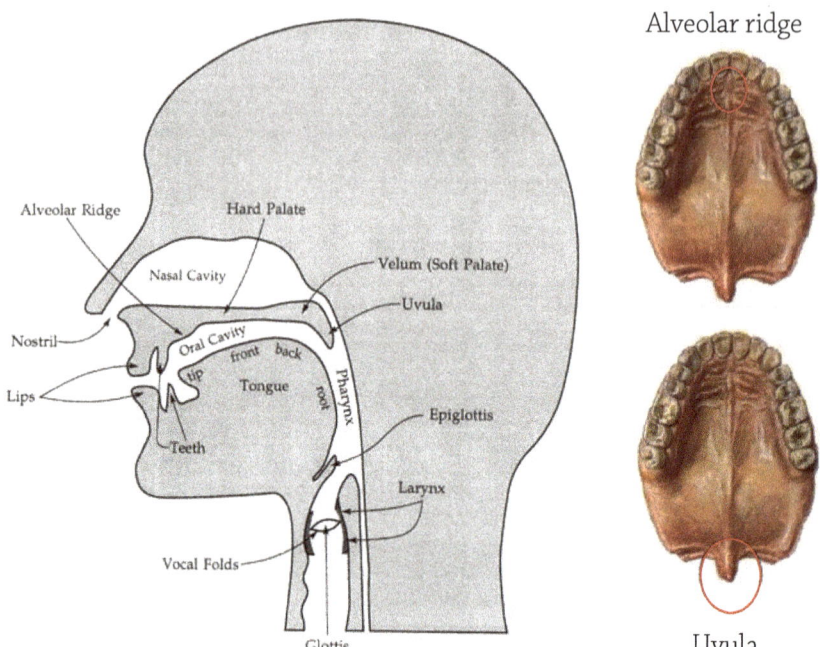

To identify the place and manner of articulation of consonants, we first need to look again at anatomy. Above is a diagram of the *articulators* - or all of the parts used to make sounds. We talk about the relevant parts of the anatomy as the *passive (or upper) articulators* and the *active (or lower) articulators*.

The passive articulators in general don't move. These include (from front to back) the:
- top lip,
- top front teeth,
- alveolar ridge (the ridge behind the upper front teeth),
- palate (the hard part of the roof of the mouth also known as the hard palate),
- velum (the soft palate),
- uvula (the soft appendage hanging from the velum) and,
- the rear wall of the pharynx (the tube above the larynx).

The *active articulators* move up and down to make contact with the passive articulators, and include the:
- bottom lip,
- bottom front teeth, and
- tongue.

The tongue is very important in speech, and different parts of it are used to make different kinds of sounds. These include the:
- *tip* or *apex* (the most forward part of the tongue),
- *blade* (the zone just behind the tip),
- *front*, which lies below the palate when at rest,
- *back*, which lies below the velum when at rest, and
- *root* (the lowest part of the tongue in the throat)

Place of articulation

As we said, the *place of articulation* is which vocal organs are used to obstruct the flow of air when a sound is made. As you can imagine, there's a fairly large number of possible places of articulation. For now we will concentrate on the ones that you use - the main places of articulation for Australian English consonants include the following, going from the front of the mouth toward the back.
- The **bilabial** place of articulation involves the upper and lower lips. The airstream is stopped or highly obstructed by the lips being together or very near each other.
- The **labiodental** place of articulation involves the lower lip and upper front teeth.
- **Dental** sounds are made with the tip or blade of the tongue touching or being very close to the upper front teeth. Sometimes the tongue is between the upper and lower front teeth, and we can call these **interdental** sounds. Some people say the two *th* sounds of English (as in *thing* and *this*) as interdentals, but many speakers of English don't have their tongue between their teeth for these sounds, but behind and close to the upper teeth. In any case interdentals are a kind of dental sound, so we call the *th* sounds dentals.
- If the tongue tip or blade makes contact with or is very close to the alveolar ridge, we say the **alveolar** place of articulation is involved.
- If the tongue blade comes close to or touches the back of the alveolar ridge or just behind the alveolar ridge we have **palato-alveolar** sounds (some people use the term alveopalatal, but this should be avoided).
- Sounds made with the front of the tongue and the palate are called **palatal** sounds.
- Those made with the back of the tongue and the velum are **velar** sounds.
- Finally, obstruction of the glottis is called **glottal** place of articulation.

There are other places of articulation which come up in other accents of English and/or other languages. These include the following:
- **Uvular** sounds involve the back of the tongue and the uvula. These occur in

Inuktitut and Arabic, among many other languages.
- **Pharyngeal** sounds involve a narrowing of the airflow in the pharynx, and are found in Hebrew and Arabic and some other languages.

There are a number of exotic places of articulation that occur in very few languages. E.g. some languages of Vanuatu have sounds using the **linguo-labial** place of articulation, in which the tongue touches or comes close to the upper lip.

Manner of Articulation

Remember that we said *manner of articulation* is about the type and degree of obstruction of a consonant.

Oral stops

Some sounds involve total obstruction of the airstream - air is pushed out of the lungs, but one articulator moves to make contact with another to completely block air from escaping out of the mouth. After a fraction of a second the articulator moves away, and the air, which had been compressed in the mouth and/or throat, rushes out.

These are called *oral stops*, or just *stops* for short. The *b* and *p* sounds in English are stops, and they are *bilabial stops* - the air from the lungs is momentarily blocked by the two lips being together, and then it's released.

We can now fully name some sounds of English, and we'll give the IPA symbols for them as well. The name of each consonant usually has at least three parts: *voicing*, *place of articulation*, and *manner of articulation*.

So, the *p* sound as in the word *spin* is called a *voiceless bilabial stop* because of how it's made:

- It is *voiceless*, because the vocal folds are apart when the air from the lungs passes between them, so they don't vibrate.
- It is *bilabial*, because the place of articulation involves the upper and lower lips, where the airstream is stopped by the lips being together.
- It is a *stop*, because the air is completely blocked.

The symbol for it, not surprisingly, is [p].

Most consonants come in voiceless and voiced pairs and this is true here - the *b* sound as in *boy* is made just as [p] is, except that the vocal folds are close together and therefore vibrate when the air passes between them; the symbol for it is [b] and we refer to it as a *voiced bilabial stop*.

There are *stops* using other places of articulation as well. If the tip or blade of the tongue touches the alveolar ridge, it will block air that's coming from the lungs. If the vocal folds are not vibrating, it will make a *voiceless alveolar stop*; the *t* sound in the word *sting*, for which the symbol is [t].

If the vocal cords are vibrating, we have a *voiced alveolar stop* - the *d* sound in the word *dog*, and the symbol for this sound is [d].

In English there are also velar stops, with the back of the tongue touching the velum; a *voiceless velar stop*, for which the symbol is [k], occurs in the word *skin*, and a *voiced velar stop* is found at the beginning of the word *go*; the symbol for it is [g].

Nasal stops

The velum (soft palate) is movable: if it is in a lowered position, it is not touching the back of the throat. If it is raised, it is touching the back of the throat - and when that happens, air can't escape into the nasal passages and out through the nose. In fact, in all the sounds we have talked about so far, as well as in most speech sounds in general, the velum is in this raised position, so air can't escape out through the nose.

This means that for the stops like [b] and [k], while the complete obstruction is being made no air is escaping out anywhere - not out of the mouth because of the obstruction somewhere, and not out of the nose because of the position of the velum. When the obstruction is ended, air is released out the mouth, but it still can't escape out of the nose because the velum is still against the back of the throat.

However, it is possible to make a complete obstruction somewhere in the mouth, but at the same time have the velum lowered, which means that air is *only* escaping through the nose. Sounds that are made this way are called *nasal stops*, or *nasals* for short.

In English we have a *bilabial nasal*. Just as with [p] and [b], air is briefly prevented from escaping out the mouth, but it continuously goes out through the nose because the velum is lowered. The first consonant of *mother* is such a sound. As with *b* you should feel your lips together. Nasals are generally voiced, so they don't come in pairs like stops do (although voiceless nasals are possible, and occur in some languages, e.g. Burmese).

So the full name of this sound at the beginning of *mother*, is a *voiced bilabial nasal*, though we often leave out the "voiced", because we assume that nasals are voiced unless otherwise specified. The symbol for it is [m].

PHONETICS 2

There's also a *voiced alveolar nasal*, which is just like [d] except that the velum is lowered so that air flows out through the nasal passages and the nose. The symbol for it is [n] and we find it at the beginning of the word *no*.

English also has a *voiced velar nasal*. The word *sing* doesn't end with an [n] followed by a [g], it ends with a single consonant, the *velar nasal*. With the symbol for the velar nasal we have our first symbol that's not also a letter of the English alphabet - it's an *n* with a hook on the right leg turning to the left: [ŋ].

Other languages have nasals involving other places of articulation. For example, many languages such as Spanish have a *palatal nasal*, represented by [ɲ].

? DISCUSSION POINTS

1. As you think about some of the basic characteristics of language, what specific things do you see that point to a Creator, or reveal something of the character of God?

2. Think of as many words as you can that use the sounds covered so far - [p], [b], [t], [d], [k], [g], [m], [n] and [ŋ] - that differ only in that one sound (e.g. pin, bin, tin, kin, din, kim, king, etc.). Say the words aloud and think about the differences in articulation of the words. Now try saying them silently (only moving your mouth) and see if others can work out which word you are saying. Note which are the hardest words to distinguish and try to determine why.

3. How does the exercise above show the importance of accurate pronunciation in communicating a clear message?

➡ ACTIVITIES

1. Search for and watch a video online using the search terms "English Consonants Voicing and Place IPA" Try and find videos that are in a series so you can use the same series throughout this module.

2. If the IPA videos you have watched so far are part of a series, watch the next video in the series after English pronunciation of consonants voicing and place. Remember as you watch it our goals for studying phonetics - not to memorize all the sounds and know how to write them, but to become aware of the great variety of sounds that are possible in language, and that the IPA has a symbol to represent each one.

3. Review the anatomy of the vocal tract until you know the names and positions of the important articulators.

4. Which of the following combinations are not possible? (answers on the next page)

active articulator	passive articulator
lower lip	upper teeth
back of tongue	alveolar ridge
back of tongue	upper lip
back of tongue	uvula
tongue tip	hard palate
tongue blade	uvula

PHONETICS 2

> ✓ **ANSWER**
>
> Answers for 4. The following combinations are not possible:
>
> | active articulator | passive articulator |
> |---|---|
> | back of tongue | alveolar ridge |
> | back of tongue | upper lip |
> | tongue blade | uvula |

5.5 Phonetics 3

OBJECTIVES OF THIS TUTORIAL

This tutorial continues to look at the manner of articulation of various speech sounds.

Introduction

In the last tutorial we started to look at manner of articulation - the type and degree of obstruction of the airflow when consonants are made. We have already looked at the oral stops and the nasal stops. In this tutorial we will look at the *manner of articulation* of some more types of consonants.

Fricatives

With all the sounds that we've discussed so far (the *stops*) there's a brief complete obstruction of the airflow. If we bring one articulator very close to another, the airflow can pass between the two articulators but has to go through a very narrow passage, creating a kind of noise. The sounds made in this way are *fricatives*.

Usually with fricatives the velum is raised, so that air can't escape out of the nose, though it's continuously passing through the narrow passage out of the mouth. English doesn't have bilabial fricatives, though some languages, including Spanish, do.

English has *labiodental fricatives*, where the lower lip comes close to or touches the upper front teeth; the *voiceless* and *voiced labiodental fricatives* are the initial sounds in *fine* and *vine*, the symbols for them being [f] and [v] respectively.

There are two sounds in English written as <th> - as in *thing* and *this*. These are *voiceless* and *voiced dental fricatives* respectively. The IPA symbols for these are [θ] and [ð].

English also has *voiced* and *voiceless alveolar fricatives*, as in the words *sue* and *zoo* - here we bring the tip or blade of the tongue very close to the alveolar ridge - and the symbols for them are [s] and [z].

There are also palato-alveolar fricatives in English; remember that palato-alveolar sounds involve the blade of the tongue and the back of the alveolar ridge or the area just behind the alveolar ridge. The *sh* sound of *ship* is a *voiceless palato-alveolar fricative*; the symbol for it is a long, stretched out *s*: [ʃ].

We also have a *voiced palato-alveolar fricative* in English, but it's rare; it's the sound in the middle of *pleasure* and at the end of *rouge*. The symbol for it resembles the number 3, but with a flat top and part of it goes below the line of writing: [ʒ].

Finally, there's a *voiceless glottal fricative* as in the word *hat*; its symbol is [h].

Some other languages have fricatives in other places of articulation. For example, German has a voiceless velar fricative, as in the word *Buch* 'book'; it also occurs in Scottish English in the well known word *loch* as in the *Loch Ness monster*. This symbol is [x].

German also has a voiceless palatal fricative, also spelled with <ch> in German, as in the word *ich* - meaning 'I'. The symbol for this is [ç].

Affricates

Remember what we said about *stops* - that they involve a brief complete blockage of the airflow, then one articulator moves away from the other and the compressed air behind the blockage rushes out. The air rushes out because the articulator moves away quickly.

If the articulator moves away slowly, the formerly blocked air can still escape, but only through a narrow passage, since the articulator has yet not moved far enough away for the air flow to be completely free. The sound created - when there is a complete blockage followed by a gradual release - is called an *affricate*.

The symbols for affricates are made up of a symbol for a stop followed by the symbol for a fricative, which is appropriate, since affricates could be seen as sequences of a stop followed by a fricative.

There are only two affricates in English, a *voiceless palato-alveolar affricate* - the word *church* both begins and ends with this sound and the symbol for it is [tʃ], and a *voiced palato-alveolar affricate* - the name *George* begins and ends with this sound, for which the symbol is [dʒ].

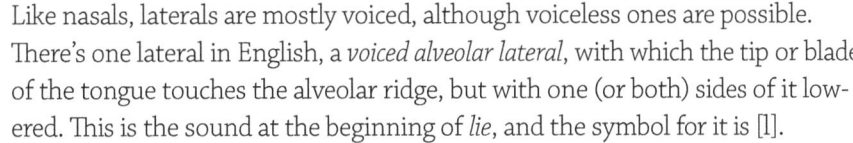

Other affricates can be found in some other languages, for example Russian and Japanese both have a voiceless alveolar affricate [ts] as in the words *tsar* and *tsunami*.

Laterals

We can put our tongue against various places on the upper surface of the mouth and completely block the flow of air, creating a stop. If we lower one or both sides of the tongue while doing this, the air will be able to flow out around the sides of the tongue, although it's blocked from going out the centre of the mouth by the tongue against some other articulator. This is the *lateral* manner of articulation.

Like nasals, laterals are mostly voiced, although voiceless ones are possible. There's one lateral in English, a *voiced alveolar lateral*, with which the tip or blade of the tongue touches the alveolar ridge, but with one (or both) sides of it lowered. This is the sound at the beginning of *lie*, and the symbol for it is [l].

Approximants

Approximant is another manner of articulation, in which two articulators are close together, but not as close as for a fricative, so there's no fricative noise. Approximants are generally voiced, but voiceless ones are possible. English has two kinds of approximants: rhotics and glides.

Rhotic approximants

Different languages and dialects have different 'r'-type sounds, representing several manners of articulation. Together these are called *rhotics*.

The *r* sound of Australian English (as in the word *red*) is made by bringing the tip or blade of the tongue fairly close to the alveolar ridge, but not so close as to create a noisy airflow. We call this sound a *voiced alveolar approximant*. The symbol for this sound is an upside-down backwards letter *r*, [ɹ].

Another 'r'-type sound that occurs in the speech of some speakers of English is a *tap* (tap is a manner of articulation). When some speakers say the words *latter* and *ladder*, there is not a *t* sound (or a *d*-sound) in the middle of the words. They are actually saying another sound, which involves the tongue quickly moving up from its rest position to strike the alveolar ridge and coming down again, it's sort of like a flicking motion. The symbol for it is [ɾ]. It's voiced, so we call it a *voiced alveolar tap*.

Some speakers of English, and some other languages have yet another 'r'-type sound, a *trill*. With this manner of articulation one articulator is held loosely near another so that the flow of air between them sets them in motion, alternately sucking them together and blowing them apart. Trills are distinctive sounds; Spanish has an alveolar trill, and this is what the IPA symbol [r] stands for. It is also found in some dialects of English, like Scottish English.

Glides

We mentioned glides before, and said that they sound like vowels but are used like consonants. If you look at the IPA chart, you will see that glides are classified as approximants.

The sound which begins the word *yes* involves bringing the front of the tongue (the part behind the tip and blade of the tongue) towards the palate - not touching the palate, for then we would have a stop, nor even close enough to cause a noisy air flow, but just relatively close. This sound is a *voiced palatal approximant*. The IPA symbol for it is [j]

Sometimes an IPA symbol is not what we would expect it to be, as in the one above, but the letter <j> is used to spell this sound in German, e.g. *ja* 'yes'. There *is* an IPA symbol [y] but it stands for a vowel, not this glide sound.

As well as [ɹ] and [j] there's one more approximant in Australian English, a more complicated one: the back of the tongue is raised toward the velum, though not enough to block the air flow or make it noisy. And at the same time the lips are rounded. All this creates the *w* sound of English, as in *we*. Because it involves both the lips and the back of the tongue and the velum in the IPA chart this sound is called *labiovelar* (or sometimes *labial-velar*). The IPA symbol for it is [w].

(Answers for questions 4 - 34 are available at the end. Complete as much as you can on your own first, by remembering, or looking up the tutorial notes, before checking your answers. Submit your answers and any corrections.)

TUTORIAL 5.5

➡ ACTIVITIES

1. Review the video on consonants that you watched for the last tutorial.
2. Review a chart of vocal tract anatomy before doing the next exercises.
3. In the table below are listed all the symbols for the consonants we use in Australian English, showing their place and manner of articulation.
   - Find them on an interactive IPA chart online and listen to how each one sounds.
   - After you listen to each sound, say it yourself, then think about what the place and manner of articulation are for that particular sound. Say it again and take note of where in the mouth it is made, and what is physically taking place for you to make that particular sound.

Manner and Place of articulation of Australian English Consonants

Manner of Articulation	Place of Articulation							
	Bilabial	Labiodental	Dental	Alveolar	Palatoalveolar	Palatal	Velar	Glottal
Stop								
voiceless	p			t			k	ʔ
voiced	b			d			g	
Affricate								
voiceless					tʃ			
voiced					dʒ			
Fricative								
voiceless		f	θ	s	ʃ			h
voiced		v	ð	z	ʒ			
Nasal	m			n			ŋ	
Lateral				l				
Approximant								
rhotic				ɹ				
glide	w					j		

- Look at this second chart, with examples of Australian English consonants. Think of other words that are examples of each sound.

PHONETICS 3

Examples of Australian English Consonants

Stops		Fricatives		Affricates	
p	pin	f	fat	tʃ	choke
b	bin	v	vat	dʒ	joke
t	tin	θ	thing		
d	din	ð	then		
k	curl	s	seal		
g	girl	z	zeal		
		ʃ	shoe		
		ʒ	treasure		
		h	hat		

Nasals		Approximants		Laterals	
m	mat	ɹ	rat	l	leaf
n	no	j	yes		
ŋ	ring	w	with		

4. Which of these words begin with a bilabial consonant? *mat gnat sat bat rat pat*

5. Which of these words begin with a velar consonant? *knot got lot cot hot pot*

6. Which of these words begin with a labiodental consonant? *fat cat that mat chat vat*

7. Which of these words begin with an alveolar consonant? *zip nip lip sip tip dip*

8. Which of these words begin with a dental consonant? *pie guy shy thigh thy high*

9. Which of these words begin with a palato-aveolar consonant? *sigh shy tie thigh thy lie*

10. Which of these words end with a fricative? *race wreath bush bring breathe bang rave real ray rose rough*

11. Which of these words end with a nasal? *rain rang dumb deaf*

12. Which of these words end with a stop? *pill lip lit graph crab dog hide laugh back*

13. Which of these words begin with a lateral? *nut lull bar rob one*

14. Which of these words begin with an approximant? *we you one run*

15. Which of these words end with an affricate? *much back edge ooze*

16. In of these which words is the consonant in the middle *voiced*? tracking mother robber leisure massive stomach razor

Name the consonant sounds in the middle of each of the following words as indicated in the example:

    robber   *voiced bilabial stop*

17. father
18. singing
19. etching
20. ether
21. pleasure
22. hopper
23. selling
24. sunny
25. lodger
26. adder

Following are some groups of words. Considering one group at a time, pronounce the words (as many times as necessary) and compare the sounds that the bold letter(s) in each word stands for (ignore the rest of the word). Are all 5 sounds in the 5 words the same? If so, write "All the same." Find one other word that includes this same sound. Are four of the sounds the same and one different, or are three of the sounds the same and two different? If so, make a note of the words whose relevant sounds don't match those of the others in that group. For these words, find one example of another word that has the same sound. Also, find an example word with the same sound that's included in the other words in that group. Remember: sameness or difference in spelling is irrelevant.

27.	**28.**	**29.**	**30.**
sh rink	th umb	smoo ch ing	tac t
bi sh op	bo th	smu dge	walk ed
na t ion	e th er	ge nerous	wait ed
spe c ial	o th er	le g end	rac ed
spla sh	th at	J une	logg ed

31. Make a list of English words (in normal orthography) in which the sounds below appear in the following positions:
- initial - at the beginning
- medial - in the middle, and
- final - at the end.

$$[z]\ [t]\ [p]\ [l]\ [k]\ [ʃ]\ [f]\ [b]\ [m]\ [n]\ [s]\ [θ]$$

Give the phonetic symbol and the three-term articulatory description (i.e. voicing, place of articulation, and manner of articulation) for the first and last sound of each of the following words:

		Symbol	Description
32. *soothe*	first sound		
	last sound		
33. *gym*	first sound		
	last sound		
34. *cough*	first sound		
	last sound		

4. These words begin with a bilabial consonant: *mat bat pat*

✓ ANSWER

5. These words begin with a velar consonant: *got cot*
6. These words begin with a labiodental consonant: *fat vat*
7. These words begin with an alveolar consonant: *zip nip lip sip tip dip*
8. These words begin with a dental consonant: *thigh thy*
9. This word begins with a palato-alveolar consonant: *shy*
10. These words end with a fricative: *race wreath bush breathe rave rose rough*
11. These words end with a nasal: *rain rang dumb*
12. These words end with a stop: *lip lit crab dog hide back*
13. This word begins with a lateral: *lull*
14. These words begin with an approximant: *we you one run*
15. These words end with an affricate: *much edge*
16. These are the words in which the consonant in the middle is voiced: *mother robber leisure stomach razor*
17. father   *voiced dental fricative* [ð]
18. singing   *voiced velar nasal* [ŋ]
19. etching   *voiceless palato-alveolar affricate* [tʃ]
20. ether   *voiceless dental fricative* [θ]
21. pleasure   *voiced palato-alveolar fricative* [ʒ]
22. hopper   *voiceless bilabial stop* [p]
23. selling   *voiced alveolar lateral* [l]
24. sunny   *voiced alveolar nasal* [n]
25. lodger   *voiced palato-alveolar affricate* [dʒ]
26. adder   *voiced alveolar tap* [ɾ]
27. All the same - other examples: se*ss*ion, fa*sh*ion, mo*t*ion, *sh*eer.
28. *th*umb, bo*th*, e*th*er (all voiceless dental fricatives) - other examples: *th*ing, tee*th*. o*th*er, *th*at (these two are voiced dental fricatives) - other examples: nei*th*er, *th*is.
29. smoo*ch*ing (is a voiceless palato-alveolar affricate) - other examples: *ch*eese, cat*ch*ing, *ch*eer.

(the other four are voiced palato-alveolar affricates) - other examples: *ja*w, e*dge*, fri*dge*.

30. ta*ct*, wal*ked*, ra*ced* (voiceless alveolar stops) - other examples: finish*ed*, sen*t*, minu*t*e. wait*ed*, log*ged* (voiced alveolar stops) - other examples: frie*d*, smelle*d*.

31. The table below shows examples of English words (in normal orthography) in which the following sounds appear in initial (at the beginning), medial (in the middle), and final (at the end), position:

Sound	Initial position	Medial position	Final position
[z]	zoo, xylophone	sizes, prizes, easy	dogs, beds, she's, buzz
[t]	top, taken, ten	better, lighting, subtle	cat, halt, finished
[p]	put, panic, pie	apple, pepper, topic	cup, stop
[l]	let, languid, look	follow, silly, always	still, idol
[k]	can, crayon, kite	speaker, making	stick, shock, mimic
[ʃ]	she, chamois, shine	station, crushing	push, mash
[f]	food, freeze, physical	offer, coffee, telephone	safe, staff, tough
[b]	boy, baggage, bad	baby, webbing, table	rob, cab
[m]	make, minimum	summer, mimic	time, mum, forum
[n]	nose, know, no	under, enough, dinner	known, thin
[s]	snip, sit, city	senses, passing	cats, face, ice
[θ]	thick, thirsty	nothing, breathy	teeth, breath

[z] [t] [p] [l] [k] [ʃ] [f] [b] [m] [n] [s] [θ]

			Symbol	Description
32.	*soothe*	first sound	[s]	*voiceless alveolar fricative*
		last sound	[ð]	*voiced dental fricative*
33.	*gym*	first sound	[dʒ]	*voiced palato-alveolar affricate*
		last sound	[m]	*voiced bilabial nasal*
34.	*cough*	first sound	[k]	*voiceless velar stop*
		last sound	[f]	*voiceless labiodental fricative*

5.6 Phonetics 4

OBJECTIVES OF THIS TUTORIAL

This tutorial introduces the vowel sounds. We will see how vowels are classified according to how they are formed in the mouth when they are said. We will also see where the particular vowel sounds of Australian English are represented on the IPA chart.

Introduction to Vowels

Remember that we said the difference between consonants and vowels is that consonants involve a significant obstruction of the airflow, but vowels don't. This means that *place of articulation* and *manner of articulation* don't apply to vowels, since those terms refer to an obstruction of the airflow.

So vowels are classified differently to consonants, and they are charted in a separate diagram on the IPA for that reason. We classify vowels on the basis of three factors - two are to do with the position of tongue - *height* and *backness* - and one has to do with the shape of the lips - *rounding*. We will be looking at these factors below.

Voicing also applies to vowels; they can be voiced or voiceless. However, because vowels are normally voiced, we don't bother mentioning voicing when we describe vowels. You should be aware though, that in some languages there are voiceless vowels.

Height, backness and rounding

When we make a vowel sound, our tongue is in a particular position to make that particular sound - it is at a certain *height* in the mouth, and at a certain place *forward or backward* in the mouth.

There are 3 degrees of *backness*: **front**, **central**, and **back**.

There are 4 degrees of *height*: **high**, **mid-high**, **mid-low**, and **low** (also called **close, close-mid, open-mid,** and **open**).

As well as backness and height of the tongue, another factor that effects which vowel sound is made is the shape of the lips. There are two basic lip shapes, **rounded** and **unrounded**.

Say the words "Oh, no!" - notice the shape of your lips - they are *rounded*.

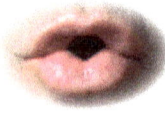

Now say the words "It is!" - now your lips are *unrounded*.

The name of every vowel will include its height, backness, and roundedness. For example, the vowel in the word *see* is referred to as *a high front unrounded vowel*.

The Vowel Chart

Vowels are represented on the *vowel chart* - you can see the IPA vowel chart below. This is not just a table - it is actually a schematic representation of the inside of the mouth - the way the vowels are laid out on the chart corresponds to their height, backness and rounding (see the diagram at right).

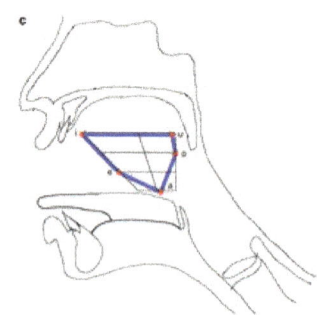

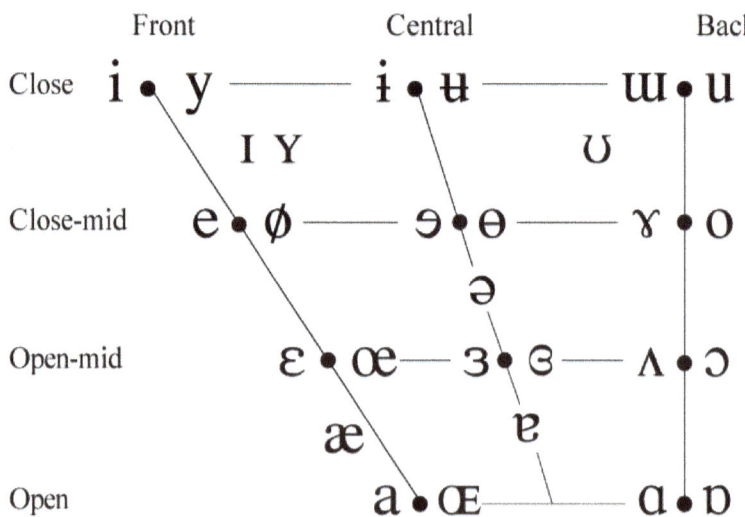

Where symbols appear in pairs, the one to the right represents a rounded vowel.

All vowels in all languages can be plotted somewhere on the vowel chart. Of course, no language has vowels in *all* the positions marked on the chart, and vowels can fall somewhere between the main vowel positions as well. For example, in Australian English we do not have vowels in the very low front position [a], but we do have the vowel [æ], which is produced somewhere between low front [a] and low-mid front [ɛ].

Each individual dialect has a *limited and specific set of vowels* that are consistent in that dialect. Each vowel sound is represented by a specific IPA symbol - one vowel sound has only one symbol - so that when you see a particular symbol, you know exactly which sound it represents in that dialect. We are going to focus only on the vowels in Australian English for now - identifying which particular vowels are used in that dialect.

Some vowels used in Australian English are not the same as American English or British English. The difference in vowels is one of the main reasons we hear different English "accents" - British, American, Scottish, Australian.

Front vowels

The first vowel we will look at is the vowel sound in *see*, *he*, and *leap* (note that this sound is spelled in a couple different ways in English). This vowel is made at the highest point of the tongue for a vowel, and also at the most forward point of the tongue that's used for making vowels. The lips are unrounded, which is why we call it *high front unrounded*. The symbol for it is [i]. You must be careful with the symbols for vowels, since they often don't stand for what you might expect them to stand for: [i] stands for the vowel sound in *see*, *he*, and *leap* and not the vowel in *bit*.

Now let's think about the vowel in the word *pet*, *bed* and *met*. The front of the tongue is still raised, but not as much as for the vowel in *see*. The lips again are unrounded. We call this vowel a *mid-low front unrounded vowel*, and the symbol for it is [ɛ].

Some people use the letter <e> as the symbol for the vowel in *bet*, i.e. [e], and if you look at the IPA chart you'll see that this symbol corresponds to a *mid-high front unrounded vowel*. The reason for the use of different symbols is that this vowel falls between the mid-high and mid-low levels, and in some accents of English it's higher than in others; which symbol a phonetician uses depends on which accent of English he is describing.

Another front vowel is the vowel sound in the words *bat* and *glad* (in Australian English). If you look at the IPA chart you'll see that it's quite low, though not at the bottom of the chart, and we can refer to it as a *low front unrounded vowel*. The symbol for it is an <a> and an <e> joined together: [æ].

If you look the IPA vowel chart you'll see that there's a completely low front unrounded vowel, the vowel that has a printed letter <a> as a symbol: [a]. Technically this is the *low front unrounded vowel*, but because we don't have this in Australian English we use that same description for [æ].

The highest point of the tongue when making the vowel sound in the word *hit* is quite high, but not quite as high as that of [i]; it's between the heights of [i] and [e]. Some people call it a semi-high vowel. You can see from the IPA vowel chart that it's also not quite as far forward as [i]. The symbol for this sound is [ɪ] - a small capital letter <I>.

NOTE: The IPA uses several capital letters as symbols. When you are transcribing phonetically, you shouldn't use capital letters (at the beginnings of sentences or for names) unless you mean to indicate the sound for which the capital letter stands.

Central vowels

Look on the chart and you will see the low central vowel, is [ɐ]. When we say this sound, the highest point of the tongue is between the front and the back. In Australian English, it occurs in words like *card* and *far* (note that there's no *r*-sound in these words, in spite of the spelling). Although this vowel is [ɐ] on the chart, the usual way of representing it for Australian English is [a].

Australian English also has another low central vowel - the vowel in *cut*. This is usually represented using the symbol [ʌ] (called 'caret'). You will notice that on the IPA chart, this symbol is supposed to represent a mid-low back unrounded vowel. In Australian English, this vowel is actually said with the tongue further forward (not as far back), but the symbol [ʌ] is used for this particular Australian English vowel.

For these two low central vowels, the mouth is in a close position for both of them - we can call them both low central, but: [ʌ] is a *lax* low central unrounded vowel while [a] is a *tense* low central unrounded vowel. The mouth is slightly more tense when saying [a].

There is an open-mid (i.e. mid-low) unrounded vowel, the symbol for it is [ɜ] (it looks a bit like the number 3, but it's not). It occurs in the words *herd* and *word*; note again that there's no *r*-sound in these words, in spite of the spelling, and that different letters are used to spell this sound in English.

Just above this vowel in the chart is an upside-down backwards letter <e>:[ə]. This is a very common vowel of English; it's called the *schwa*. It occurs in many unstressed syllables (we'll discuss stress in the next tutorial) - it is in the first syllable of the word *above*. Schwa never occurs in stressed syllables in English. You'll see that it's right in the middle of the vowel chart, and it's unrounded, so we call it a *mid central unrounded vowel*.

Schwa and [ɜ] are in close positions to each other in the vowel chart, and we can use the tense/lax distinction again, and call them both mid: [ɜ] is a *tense mid central unrounded* vowel while schwa is a *lax mid central unrounded* vowel.

Now let's look at high central vowels. In many dialects of English the vowel in words like *blue* is a high back rounded vowel, for which the symbol is [u]. This is the symbol used for this vowel in Australian English, even though it is not strictly accurate. In Australian English, the vowel in words like *blue* is produced by most speakers as a high *central* rounded vowel (for which the correct symbol is a [ʉ], or "barred u"). There are no high central *unrounded* vowels in Australian English, but if you're familiar with New Zealand English you'll know the distinctive vowel occurring in *fish*. This vowel is a high central unrounded vowel, and the symbol is a "barred i", [ɨ].

Back vowels

In many dialects of English the vowel in *blue* is the high back rounded vowel [u], but as we just saw, in Australian English it is usually central, so we use the [u] symbol for our high *central* rounded vowel. Look on the chart and you will see there's a vowel in a position a little lower than [u], for which the symbol is [ʊ]. This is the sound in the words *book* and *put* (note once again the same sound is represented in more than one way in English spelling).

The vowel in the English words *caught*, *raw*, *port*, and *bought* is also a back vowel. In many dialects it is considerably lower (i.e. the highest part of the tongue is not very high) - it's a *mid-low back rounded vowel*, and the symbol for it is [ɔ], which looks like a backwards <c>. In Australian English this vowel is actually said higher – it is a *mid-high back rounded vowel*, (for which the correct IPA symbol is [o]). However, the symbol used for Australian English for this sound is usually [ɔ].

Australian English also has a *low back rounded vowel*, the vowel in *cot* (American English has a different vowel here), and the symbol for it is [ɒ], which looks like a backwards version of the letter <a> when you write it.

Diphthongs

All of the vowels that we've looked at so far have something in common - whatever tongue and lip position they have had, they have kept the same throughout their duration - they don't change part of the way through saying them. But, there are also vowels that *do* change tongue and/or lip position. The tongue and/or lips move from one position to another. These vowels are called *diphthongs* and there are several of them in Australian English. (Vowels that do not change are called *monophthongs*.)

The symbols for diphthongs are easy, they are made up of the symbol for the vowel representing the initial position followed by the symbol for the vowel representing the final position.

Three Australian English diphthongs have [ɪ] as their end point. These are *front raising diphthongs*:

PHONETICS 4

- In the vowel in the word *bay* the tongue starts out in the position of [e] and ends in the position for [ɪ], and so the symbol for it is [eɪ].
- the vowel in the word *buy* involves a movement from the position of [a] and ends in [ɪ] and the symbol for it is [aɪ].
- the vowel in the word *boy* starts out with the tongue and lip position for [ɔ] and moves to the position for [ɪ], and thus the symbol for it is [ɔɪ].

Two other Australian English diphthongs have [ʊ] as their end point. These are *back raising diphthongs*:

- [aʊ] as in *how*,
- and [oʊ] as in *low* and *toe*.

There are three other diphthongs in Australian English, where the tongue moves toward the mid central position of schwa, [ə]: These are called *centering diphthongs*.

- [ɪə] as in *here*, *beer*, and *near*,
- [ɛə] as in *bear*, *care*, and *hair*,
- and [ʊə] as in *lure*. (Note there's no 'r' sound in these words, and again these sounds are represented in more than one way in English spelling.)

A Summary of Vowels in Australian English

Conventional symbols used (Macquarie Dictionary)

Simple vowels (Monophthongs)		Diphthongs	
heed	i	buy	aɪ
hid	ɪ	bay	eɪ
head	ɛ	boy	ɔɪ
had	æ	how	aʊ
hard	a	hoe	oʊ
hut	ʌ	here	ɪə
hot	ɒ	hair	ɛə
hoard	ɔ	lure	ʊə
hood	ʊ		
who'd	u		
above	ə		
heard	ɜ		

ACTIVITIES

1. Do some research online about the changes in Australian English (specifically focusing on pronunciation and phonetics) over the decades.

2. Try and find some video/audio clips of Australians speaking in past decades. Listen to how the Australian English dialect has changed. Think about which particular vowel sounds have changed.

3. Now you have learned all the symbols for the sounds of Australian English, you can try some phonetic transcription for yourself. Transcribe the fifty words below, using the IPA symbols you learned for consonants and vowels. Say the word several times, then transcribe it using broad transcription (no need to write diacritics or stress markers.) Once you have attempted to phonetically transcribe all the words, check your answers on the page following. If you have made a mistake or had trouble with particular sounds or symbols, review the notes on those sounds.

1. car
2. eat
3. map
4. role
5. boy
6. fine
7. thought
8. purse
9. youth
10. beige
11. jog
12. then
13. cheers
14. tin
15. dare
16. shove
17. hang
18. mouse
19. wash
20. fade
21. tax
22. tenth
23. pride
24. creep
25. dwell
26. taps
27. link
28. caused
29. spliced
30. script
31. scrunched
32. bulged
33. crusts
34. sixths
35. strength
36. helm
37. robbed
38. cash
39. you'll
40. grasp
41. slow
42. flare
43. tired
44. wink
45. frowned
46. loins
47. stewed
48. square
49. welsh
50. hinged

(Answers on next page. Note: If you speak a different dialect of English, your transcription will be different from the answers, which are for Australian English - note the particular variations and where they differ from Australian English. Even for Australian English speakers, some vowel sounds may vary from person to person, as it is difficult to transcribe vowels consistently even within one dialect.)

PHONETICS 4

✓ ANSWERS

1. kɑ
2. it
3. mæp
4. ɹəul
5. bɔɪ
6. faɪn
7. θot
8. pɜs
9. juθ
10. bæɪʒ
11. dʒɔg
12. ðɛn
13. tʃɪəz
14. tɪn
15. dɛ
16. ʃʌv
17. hæŋ
18. mæɔs
19. wɔʃ
20. fæɪd
21. tæks
22. tɛnθ
23. pɹɑɛd
24. kɹɪp
25. dwɛl
26. tæps
27. lɪŋk
28. kozd
29. splɑɛst
30. skɹɪpt
31. skɹʌntʃt
32. baldʒd
33. kɹʌsts
34. sɪksθs
35. stɹɛŋkθ
36. helm
37. ɹɔbd
38. kæʃ
39. jul
40. gɹæsp
41. sləɹ
42. flɛ
43. tɑɛəd
44. wɪŋk
45. fɹæɔnd
46. loɪnz
47. stʃud
48. skwɛ
49. wɛlʃ
50. hɪndʒd

54

5.7 Phonetics 5

> **OBJECTIVES OF THIS TUTORIAL**
>
> This tutorial finishes the series on phonetics. We will be talking about some other factors affecting speech sounds, like tone and stress. We will also be doing some more transcription and review exercises.

Introduction

So far, we have looked at *consonants* and *vowels* and the symbols on the IPA chart that represent the particular sounds of Australian English. Now we are going to look at some other factors that affect speech sounds in particular ways, and how these secondary features are represented by marks that we add to the IPA symbols.

Some secondary features

Nasalisation

Remember that the velum (soft palate) can be up or down. It is up against the back wall of the throat when making stops like [b] and down when making nasals like [m]. When it is up, air is prevented from going out the nasal passages and nose, and when it is down, air can escape through the nasal passages. During the making of the vowels that we discussed in the last tutorial, the velum is up, meaning that air can't get out through the nose, though it can escape through the mouth, since vowels don't involve any obstruction of the airflow.

It is possible to lower the velum when making a vowel, meaning that air could get out through both the mouth and the nose. A vowel that's made when the velum is lowered is referred to as a *nasalised* vowel.

When we want to say something extra about a sound, something that usually doesn't apply to it, we often add a little mark above or below the symbol. A mark like this is called a *diacritic*. The way we mark nasalisation is by adding a diacritic, in this case a wavy line, called a *tilde*, over the symbol of the vowel involved.

PHONETICS 5

ũ For example [ũ] is a nasalised tense high back rounded vowel. Nasalisation is *predictable* in English: a vowel that occurs before a nasal consonant in the same syllable is nasalised; other vowels are not nasalised. We say that nasalisation is predictable in English because it *always and only* occurs before nasal consonants - so we can accurately predict when it will occur. For example - *beat* is [bit], but *bean* is [bĩn]. Say these two words and listen to the difference in how you say the vowel - in the second one, the velum is lowered and air is escaping through the mouth and nose.

In many other languages, nasalisation is distinctive - it isn't predictable. For example, in French *beau* is [bo], but *bon* is [bõ] - the only difference is the nasalisation of the vowel sound. Because nasalisation is predictable in English we often don't mark it in broad transcriptions.

The voiceless diacritic

Some types of sound are usually voiced, including nasals, laterals, and vowels. But in some languages these sounds can also be voiceless. Japanese has voiceless vowels. To mark such a sound as voiceless, we place a diacritic in the form of a little circle under its symbol, so [u̥] is the symbol for a voiceless tense high back rounded vowel.

Some other languages have voiceless nasals, and/or laterals, and/or rhotics. Burmese has voiceless nasals. We use the voiceless diacritic under the symbol for the particular sound - for example, [n̥] represents a voiceless alveolar nasal.

Aspiration

Another issue to do with voicing can apply to some consonants – specifically to *stop* consonants. What we find in some situations is that when a stop comes immediately before a sound that would normally be voiced, the voicing (vocal cord vibration) doesn't start immediately, but is delayed. During this delay, a puff of air comes out of the mouth. This delay in voicing is called *aspiration*. The symbol for aspiration is a small raised <h> after the symbol for the stop involved.

For example in the word *tap*, we start with a [t], which is voiceless, but then there is a vowel, and vowels are usually voiced, but in this word the voicing doesn't start until a little time after the vowel begins. Say the word and you will hear the puff of air after the [t] sound. We say that the word *tap* begins with an *aspirated stop*, (specifically an aspirated voiceless alveolar stop), and we would write it as [tʰ].

In English the only sounds that are aspirated are [p], [t], and [k], and they're only aspirated in one situation, when they're the first segment in a stressed syllable (we'll talk about segments and stress soon). For example, the [k] in *kind* is aspirated, so we would write the symbol for it as [kh], but the [k] in *skin* is not, because it's not the first sound of the syllable, and the [p] of *stop* is not aspirated either. Because aspiration is predictable in English, we often don't mark it when doing a broad transcription.

Suprasegmental features

The properties that we've been talking about so far, like the places and manners of articulation, voicing, and aspiration in consonants, or frontness and roundedness in vowels, are all features of *individual sounds*.

You can say that a particular sound is bilabial or voiced or rounded. You would not usually say that a *syllable* was rounded. However, there are some features that aren't properties of individual sounds, but properties of whole syllables, or words, or even of phrases and sentences. These kinds of features are known as *suprasegmental features*.

We are going to talk more about syllables later, but you know basically what a syllable is – for example the word *marker* has two syllables, but the word *post* has one.

Stress

One of the suprasegmental features is *stress*. If you say any English word of two or more syllables to yourself, then you'll notice that one of the syllables stands out more than the others. For example, in the following words the syllable that stands out more than the others is marked with a thing like an apostrophe: *unin'tentional*, *abo'litionist*, *compo'sition*. The syllable after the mark is the one that stands out - this is the stressed syllable.

A *stressed* syllable is one on which more energy is expended; this often means that it's louder, sometimes it differs in pitch, and sometimes it's longer. Stress is an important feature of English because sometimes different words differ only in which syllable is stressed: compare for example the noun *'permit* (an official document of authorisation) with the verb *per'mit* (to give authorisation or consent to someone).

In English, which syllable is stressed is not easily predictable; but in some other languages it is usually predictable and regular. For example, in Turkish, stress is usually predictable and there's a simple rule for it: the last syllable of a word is usually the syllable with stress. In Standard Fijian it is also predictable - the second last syllable is usually stressed, unless the last syllable has a diphthong or a long vowel, in which case that syllable is stressed.

In the IPA stress is marked by a short raised vertical line, as in these words - *in'surance*, *'final*, *senti'mental*, *con'sent* - (here we have used English spelling, but generally we would be using this marker in a transcription with IPA symbols). It is possible to mark a couple of different levels of stress, but we will only worry about primary stress - marking the syllable of a word that the *most* energy is expended on.

Intonation

If you listen carefully you'll notice that the *pitch* of the voice is constantly going up and down in English sentences, and that sentences have a sort of melody. In English, and in all other languages, the pitch pattern of phrases and sentences is used to give certain kinds of information. For example, you can make a statement into a question simply by changing its pitch pattern: compare "He's here." to "He's here?" Or, "You're going today." to "You're going today?" Such pitch patterns and changes are referred to as *intonation*.

Tone

In many languages, like Chinese and Thai, pitch is also used in another way: words can have the same segments but differ in their pitches (not absolute pitches, as with music, but their pitch relative to one another) – this use of pitch is called *tone*. Tonal languages are extremely common in Africa and East Asia. Tones are used in different ways in different languages - sometimes the contour (shape) of the tone is important, sometimes the tone is the same for an entire word, or is different for each syllable. A language that is considered to be a *tonal language* is one that uses tone to convey meaning - for example, Mandarin Chinese has five distinct tones, so the same segment can have five different meanings depending on the tone used: mā "mum/mom", má "hemp", mǎ "horse", mà "scold", ma (a question marker).

The Syllable

We've been talking in terms of segments and we've discussed features, which segments are composed of, but of course there are larger units of speech, like words, phrases, and *syllables*. It has proven quite difficult to come up with a universally agreed upon definition of the syllable, but we all have some intuitive notion of the syllable, and we usually agree about how many syllables a word has (although it's sometimes more difficult to decide on the boundaries between syllables in a word).

Many languages have a writing system that's based on the segments of the language, like the English alphabet. But some languages have *syllabic* writing systems, in which symbols generally stand not for segments, but for whole syllables. Inuktitut (spoken in northern Canada) has a syllabic writing system; the writing system of ancient Babylonian was also largely syllabic.

We use the Greek letter sigma, σ, to stand for a syllable.

Syllables have internal structure:
- The "core" of a syllable is called the *nucleus*; every syllable must have a nucleus, and it's usually a vowel.

- Anything in the syllable after the nucleus is the *coda* - there will only be consonants in it.
- The nucleus and the coda together make up the *rhyme*.
- Anything in the syllable before the nucleus is the *onset*; only consonants will be found in the onset.
- A syllable can consist only of the nucleus (it doesn't have to have an onset or coda).

For example the English word *plant* consists of a single syllable. In the diagram this syllable has been broken up into its onset (any consonants preceding the vowel) and its rhyme (all sounds from the vowel to the end of the syllable). The rhyme has been further divided into the nucleus, which in the vast majority of syllables is a vowel, and the coda, which are any consonants following the nucleus.

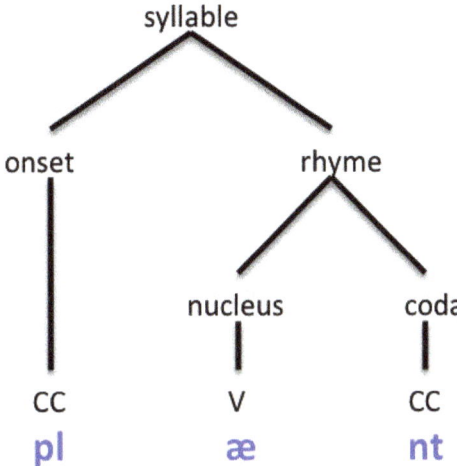

Phonotactics

Languages differ in which sounds they have, but they also differ in where in syllables sounds can occur, and what combinations can occur in different places in syllables. The rules that govern this are called *phonotactic* rules, and every language has them.

Languages differ a lot in their phonotactic rules. English is more free than some languages, though not as free as others. English allows syllables to begin with two consonants (to have two consonants in the onset), which not all languages permit - there are some languages like Hawaiian, in which you can only ever have one consonant in the onset.

Phonotactic rules not only say *how many* segments you can have in a particular place in the syllable, they also say *which* segments you can have there. Although English allows sequences of two consonants in the onset, it doesn't permit just any combination of consonants there; in fact it's quite restrictive. For example, the sequences [kn] and [pn] are not allowed to occur syllable-initially (remember we are not talking about spelling, but sequences of phonetic sounds).

English also allows three consonants in onsets, but not just *any* combination of three consonants; in fact, the first one will always have to be [s], the second one must be a voiceless stop, and the third one must be a liquid or a glide (e.g. strike, splayed). This is a phonotactic rule of English. English doesn't allow onsets with more than three consonants, but there are languages that do.

There are also restrictions about what can appear in the codas of syllables. For example in English a syllable can end in the sequence [pt], as in the word *apt*, but they cannot end in the sequence [tp]. Also, there are interesting rules about where certain sounds can occur. The velar nasal, [ŋ], is not a rare sound in English, we find it in words like *sing* and *ring*, but it is never at the beginning of a syllable in English. In other languages, such as Ata (PNG) it is quite common to have [ŋ] at the onset of syllables, such as in most of the syllables in the sentence for "you (pl) go and sleep" - *ngingi ngalai ngai*.

Because these rules exist, we can talk about *possible* words of English or another language - words that don't exist but could - as they don't violate the phonotactic rules of the language.

For example, there's no such word as *blit* in English, but there could be (maybe the name of a new product), while the word *bnit* is not a possible word of English, because it breaks the rules.

There are some universal phonotactic rules as well - there are sequences of sounds in particular places in syllables that no language allows. One example of this is the sequence [lp] which is rarely or never found in syllable onsets.

TUTORIAL 5.7

ACTIVITIES

1. Write stress markers in the correct places for the following words according to the definition given (answers on the next page):
- object - a thing, article, item or device (noun)
- object - to lodge a protest against (verb)
- subject - topic, issue, question or concern (noun)
- subject - put through, treat with or expose to (verb)
- digest - absorb, take in, understand or comprehend (verb)
- digest - compilation, synopsis or summary (noun)

2. Look at the following English words that have been adapted to fit Japanese phonotatic rules. From looking at the way the words have been adapted, try to work out the phonotatic rules of Japanese (answers on following page).

English	Japanese
Let's [speak] English!	Retsu ingurishu!
France	Furansu
Privacy	puraibashii
Smith	Sumisu
Table	teburu

3. Try to write out the following phonetic transcription using English spelling - (the : mark indicates a lengthened vowel - it won't affect your spelling, but when you say the word, lengthen the vowel before this symbol. This transcription also uses a 'barred u' rather than the conventional [u] and an [e] for the [ɛ] sound). The answer is on the next page, but try to do it on your own before looking.

di:p dæɔn hɪə bɑe ðə dɐ:k wo:tə lɪvd əʉld gɔləm ə smo:l slɑemi: kɹi:tʃə ɑe dəʉnt nəʉ we: hi: kæɪm fɹɔm no: hʉ: o: wɔt i: wɔz hi: wəz ə gɔləm əz dɐ:k əz dɐ:knəs əksept fə tʉ: bɪg ɹæɔnd pæɪl ɑez ɪn hɪz θɪn fæɪs hi: hæd ə lɪtl bəʉt ən i: ɹəʉd əbæɔt kwɑet kwɑeətli: ɔn ðə læɪk fo: læɪk ɪt wɔz wɑed ən di:p ən dedli: kəʉld hi: pædld ɪt wɪð lɐ:dʒ fi:t dæŋglɪŋ əʉvə ðə sɑed bɐt nevə ɹ ə ɹɪpəl dɪd i: mæɪk nɔt hi: hi: wəz lʉkɪŋ æɔt əv hɪz pæɪl læmplɑek ɑez fə blæend fɪʃ wɪtʃ hi: gɹæbd wɪð ɪz lɔŋ fɪŋgəz əz kwɪk əz θɪŋkɪŋ hi: lɑekt mi:t tʉ: gɔblən hi: θo:t gʉd wen i: kəd get ət bət hi: tʉk ke: ðæɪ nevə fæɔnd hɪm æɔt hi: dʒəs θɹɔtld əm fɹɔm bi:hɑend ɪf evə ðæɪ kæɪm dæɔn əlɔʉn eni:we: nɪə ði: edʒ əv ðə wo:tə wɑel hi: wəz pɹæɔlɪŋ əbæɔt ðæɪ seldəm dɪd fə ðæɪ hæd ə fi:lɪŋ ðət sɐmpθɪŋ ɐnplezənt wəz lɜ:kɪŋ dæɔn ðe: dæɔn ət ðə veɹi: ɹʉ:ts əv ðə mæɔntən

 **ANSWER**

1. Stress markers:
   - 'object - a thing, article, item or device (noun)
   - ob'ject - to lodge a protest against (verb)
   - 'subject - topic, issue, question or concern (noun)
   - sub'ject - put through, treat with or expose to (verb)
   - di'gest - absorb, take in, understand or comprehend (verb)
   - 'digest - compilation, *synopsis or summary (noun)*

2. Japanese phonotatic rules:

   Japanese syllables must be consonant-vowel, so words borrowed from English are adapted to fit this rule. Any consonant clusters have been split and final consonants have had a vowel added.

3. Transcription exercise:

Deep down here by the dark water lived old Gollum, a small slimy creature.
I don't know where he came from, nor who or what he was. He was a Gollum as dark as darkness, except for two big round pale eyes in his thin face. He had a little boat, and he rowed about quite quietly on the lake; for lake it was, wide and deep and deadly cold. He paddled it with large feet dangling over the side, but never a ripple did he make. Not he. He was looking out of his pale lamp-like eyes for blind fish, which he grabbed with his long fingers as quick as thinking. He liked meat too. Goblin he thought good, when he could get it; but he took care they never found him out. He just throttled them from behind, if ever they came down alone anywhere near the edge of the water, while he was prowling about. They seldom did, for they had a feeling that something unpleasant was lurking down there, down at the very roots of the mountain.

5.8 Phonology 1

OBJECTIVES OF THIS TUTORIAL

This tutorial introduces the area of phonology - *the organization of speech sounds*. We will look at what phonology is, and explain how it can help us as we work in other languages.

Introduction

Phonology is the study of how sounds are organised and used in languages.

The *phonological system* of a language includes:

- an inventory of sounds and their features, and
- rules which specify how sounds interact with each other.

Phonology is just one of several aspects of language. It is related to other aspects such as phonetics, morphology, syntax, and pragmatics. We have already covered an introduction to phonetics - below you can see the basic differences between phonetics and phonology.

Phonetics ...
Is the basis for phonological analysis.
Analyses the production of all human speech sounds, regardless of language.

Phonology ...
Is the basis for further work in morphology, syntax, discourse, and orthography design.
Analyses the sound patterns of a particular language by
- determining which phonetic sounds are significant, and
- explaining how these sounds are interpreted by the native speaker.

The goal for us here is to give you a basic understanding of the *principles* of phonology. If you eventually become the primary person developing a writing system in an unwritten language, it would be helpful for you to do further study at that time with that particular language in focus. At the end of our phonology introduction here, you will understand what phonology is, and you will understand more about how languages work.

Phonemes

Every language has a set of sounds that function as distinct sounds, and can distinguish meaning. These are called phonemes.

For example, in English [p] and [b] are *functionally* separate - they are distinct sounds that can indicate a different meaning when either one or the other is used. We can see they distinguish meaning because *pack* and *back* are two separate words with separate meanings. So are *cap* and *cab*, or *lap* and *lab*. The only way we can tell these pairs of words apart is by the sounds /p/ and /b/. We call this a *minimal pair*. A minimal pair is two words that differ in only one sound. In the Cashunahua language (Peru), a minimal pair is the two words [taka] 'liver' and [daka] 'to rest', because the only sounds that differ are the /t/ and /d/.

But there are some separate sounds in English that are not phonemes, like [p] and [pʰ] (aspirated [p]). These are distinctly different sounds, but they are not *functionally* separate in English because they don't distinguish meaning. We can use either one in a word and the meaning doesn't change - [pæk] and [pʰæk] would both be heard as ways of saying *pack*. In some other languages these same two sounds do distinguish meaning.

So, we say that in English [p] and [b] *contrast*, but that [p] and [pʰ] *don't contrast*. For sounds to contrast they need to be *separate sounds*, and also they need to *distinguish meaning*.

English has a set of sounds that contrast - but other languages have *different* contrasts. In Ata [ɹ] and [l] don't contrast, so they are not functionally separate: you can say *ialugu* or *iarugu* and it is the same word with the same meaning. In Warlpiri [p] and [b] don't contrast, so they are not functionally separate: you could say *Warlpiri* or *Warlbiri*.

In Thai [p] and [pʰ] do contrast, so they are functionally separate: *paa* 'forest' and *phaa* 'split' are separate words - they're a minimal pair.

So, as we said, sounds that are functionally distinct in a language are *phonemes*.

   In English /p/ and /b/ are separate phonemes, but [p] and [pʰ] are not.

   In Ata [ɹ] and [l] are not separate phonemes.

   In Warlpiri [p] and [b] are not separate phonemes.

   In Thai /p/ and /pʰ/ *are* separate phonemes.

Notice that when we write symbols for sounds (or phones), we write them between brackets: [b], [j], [o], but when we write the symbols for phonemes, we write them between slashes: /b/, /j/, /o/.

Phoneme inventory

Every language has a set of phonemes, or *phoneme inventory*. This is simply the set of functionally distinct sounds of the language.

Languages differ from each other in which possible speech sounds they use, and many languages have sounds that aren't used in English (clicks, velar fricatives, etc). English also has some sounds that are rare in other languages, like our affricates ([tʃ] in *church* and [dʒ] in *judge*) and dental fricatives (like [θ] in *thick* and [ð] in *this*).

But languages also differ on how many phonemes they have. English has 44 phonemes. You can download and read the chart of English phonemes - available on the website.

Rotokas (Bougainville) and Mura (Brazil) each have 11 phonemes (Rotokas has 6 consonants and five vowels, Mura has 8 consonants and 3 vowels). The !Xũ language (a Khoisan language of southern Africa) has 141 distinct phonemes: 95 consonants (including 48 different clicks), 24 simple vowels and 22 diphthongs. You can see four of the !Xũ phonemes (clicks) demonstrated here: http://youtu.be/Nz44WiTVJww

The way we find the phoneme inventory of a language is by studying the way the sounds are used and organised - phonology.

Contrast and complementary distribution

The concepts of *contrast* and *complementary distribution* are central to phonology - the analysis of sounds.

Contrast

We mentioned contrast already above - and said that when sounds are functionally different they are said to *contrast*. Let's look at some more examples of contrast in English.

pack /pæk/ vs. *back* /bæk/

Pack and *back* have quite different meanings, but the only difference between these two words is that one begins with /p/ and the other with /b/. These two sounds therefore *contrast* in English. This means they're functionally separate sounds, or separate phonemes in English.

Pack and *back* are therefore a *minimal pair* for /p/ and /b/, because they demonstrate that /p/ and /b/ are separate phonemes (they might not be in some other languages, but they are in English.)

In the same way, we can see that /t/ and /d/ are separate phonemes in English, and so

are /k/ and /g/, because we can find minimal pairs for these sounds also:
    tie /taɪ/ vs. *die* /daɪ/
    grab /gɹæb/ vs. *crab* /kɹæb/

With each pair above, the only difference between them is *voicing*: one is voiced, the other is voiceless. So, we can see that the feature of voicing is distinctive in English, at least for plosives. Adding voicing to one sound in a word can change the meaning. If we look at some other sounds, it turns out that voicing is distinctive for affricates and fricatives too:
    chore /tʃɔ/ vs. *jaw* /dʒɔ/
    fat /fæt/ vs. *vat* /væt/
    thigh /θaɪ/ vs. *thy* /ðaɪ/
    sap /sæp/ vs. *zap* /zæp/
    meshes /mɛʃəz/ vs. *measures* /mɛʒəz/

In the same way that voicing is distinctive in English, the feature of nasalisation is also contrastive in English. Look at these examples:
    ban /**b**æn/ vs. *man* /**m**æn/
    debt /**d**ɛt/ vs. *net* /**n**ɛt/
    log /lɒ**g**/ vs. *long* /lɒ**ŋ**/

These minimal pairs show that /m/ and /b/ are separate phonemes - so are /n/ and /d/ - and /ŋ/ and /g/.

Complementary distribution

As we said, English has 44 phonemes - but it actually has at least 51 different speech sounds. That is because some different speech sounds are not *functionally* separate. In other words switching them won't distinguish meaning.

We used the example before of [p] and [pʰ] which are phonetically different speech sounds and both occur in English, but they don't make a difference for meaning in English. Because they are not functionally separate, we say they are functionally part of a *single phoneme*.

These sounds that are part of one phoneme are called *allophones* of one phoneme. Usually allophones occur in different contexts, or *environments*. Let's look at some examples -

In English [p] and [pʰ] are allophones of a single phoneme:

[pʰ]	[pʰ]	[pʰ]	[p]	[p]	[p]	[p]
'person	pa'ternal	com'puter	'spot	con'spire	'stupid	'sleep

It is the same phoneme, but we could say that it changes depending on the environment it is in. Notice in the examples above that we get [pʰ] as the first sound in the first syllable of a word, and as the first sound in a syllable that isn't first but is stressed. [p] occurs everywhere else (the end of a syllable; the beginning of a syllable after /s/; the first sound in an unstressed syllable which is not the first syllable in a word).

So, in English the three *sounds*, [pʰ], [p] and [b] divide up into *phonemes* like this:

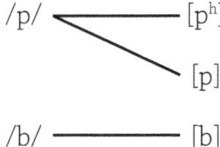

The natural reaction of a native English speaker is to say "OK, but so what? Of course they're just different ways of saying 'p'." But... that just means it seems natural to English speakers that [p] and [pʰ] are just different ways of saying what is functionally a single phoneme. Unlike /p/ and /b/, where they of course seem like functionally different sounds. But that all only seems natural because we are *English* speakers. There is nothing about these three sounds that inherently makes them divide up that way. That's just how it works in English.

Korean also has the three sounds [p], [pʰ] and [b]. But in Korean, /p/ and /pʰ/ make a difference for meaning: /pul/ 'fire' vs. /pʰul/ 'grass'. So /p/ and /pʰ/ are separate phonemes in Korean.

But also in Korean, [p] and [b] belong together: [pəp] 'law' and [mubəp] 'lawlessness'. In Korean [p] and [b] are allophones - part of the same phoneme. You get [p] at the beginning of a word and [b] between vowels.

So, in Korean the three sounds [p], [pʰ] and [b] divide up into phonemes like this:

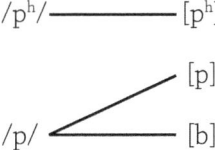

In Thai it's a different story again. Thai also has the three sounds [p], [pʰ] and [b]. But in Thai, all three make a difference for meaning: /paa/ 'forest' vs. /pʰaa/ 'split' vs. aw/baa/ 'shoulder'.

PHONOLOGY 1

So /b/, /p/ and /pʰ/ are all separate phonemes in Thai, and the three sounds divide up into phonemes like this:

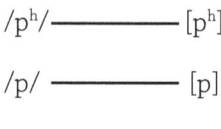

ACTIVITIES

1. Do an image search online for "The 44 Phonemes of English." Study the chart.

2. The following sets of minimal pairs show that English /b/ and /p/ contrast in initial, medial and final positions: pit/bit, rapid/rabid, cap/cab. Find similar sets of minimal pairs for each pair of consonants given below.

/k/ and /g/
/s/ and /ʃ/
/m/ and /n/
/b/ and /m/
/tʃ/ and /dʒ/
/l/ and /ɹ/
/p/ and /f/
/s/ and /z/

(possible answers on page 66)

3. Look at each of the lists of words below (from different languages). For each list, choose the set of minimal pairs that show the sounds given contrast in that language. For example, in the first list of Cambodian words, the minimal pair is [tʰae] and [tae] because the only difference in these two words is the initial sound: [t] and [tʰ].

Cambodian
- compare [t] and [tʰ]

    [tʰou] *vase*
    [tʰae] *to care for*
    [taem] *stamp*
    [tae] *but*
    [ɜae] *at*
    [taa] *grandfather*

Tidore (Indonesia)
- compare [k] and [g]

    [gasi] *salt*
    [kam] *village*
    [sako] *neck*
    [kora] *to lie*
    [sago] *to split*
    [paka] *to walk*
    [gam] *water container*

Sarangani Sangire (Philippines)
- compare [i] and [ɨ]

    [ke] *salt*
    [kɨ] *village*
    [dai] *neck*
    [bika] *to lie*
    [ki] *to split*
    [losɨ] *to walk*

Tooli (Nth. Philippines)
- compare [t] and [d]

    [kut] *we*
    [tuh] *there*
    [telem] *sharp*
    [kuda] *horse*
    [delem] *foot of hill*
    [duh] *that*

Quechua (Peru)
- compare [i] and [e]
- compare [o] and [u]

    [keru] *pole*
    [kuka] *cocaine*
    [koru] *hunchback*
    [kiru] *tooth*
    [hokta] *six*
    [peka] *head*
    [tika] *adobe*
    [hukta] *one*
    [tuku] *owl*
    [kuru] *warm*

(answers for this exercise on the next page)

 **ANSWER**

Minimal pairs (English):

/k/ and /g/ - *come / gum, ankle / angle, back / bag*

/s/ and /ʃ/ - *see / she, fist / fished, lease / leash*

/m/ and /n/ - *mitt / knit, simmer / sinner, am / an*

/b/ and /m/ - *bat / mat, grabber / grammar, cab / cam*

/tʃ/ and /dʒ/ - *chunk / junk, etching / edging, lunch / lunge*

/l/ and /ɹ/ - *lip / rip, alive / arrive, call / core*

/p/ and /f/ - *pit / fit, copy / coffee, leap / leaf*

/s/ and /z/ - *Sue / zoo, buses / buzzes, peace / peas*

Minimal pairs (other languages):

Cambodian:
　[tʰae] *to care for* / [tae] *but*

Tidore:
　[kam] *village* / [gam] *water container*

Sarangani Sangire:
　[kɨ] *village* / [ki] *to split*

Tooli:
　[telem] *sharp* / [delem] *foot of hill*

Quechua:
　[i] *and* [e]: [keru] *pole* / [kiru] *tooth*
　[o] *and* [u]: [hokta] *six* / [hukta] *one*

5.9 Phonology 2

OBJECTIVES OF THIS TUTORIAL

This tutorial continues to look at the principles of phonology. We will also be doing some basic phonological analysis exercises.

Introduction
In the last tutorial we discussed allophones. We gave an example of the same three sounds in English, Korean and Thai to show how these languages vary phonemically - how in these three languages the phonemes and their allophones are grouped differently. We could also say that the *allophonic rules* are different in these three languages.

Allophonic rules
Another example of a phonemic difference between two languages is with [l] and the *rhotic*, or 'r' sound - in English [ɹ] and Japanese [ɾ]. In English these two sounds are separate phonemes: *law* and *raw*, *lot* and *rot* are minimal pairs.

But in Japanese these two sounds are allophones of a single phoneme. If you look at the following examples of Japanese words with these two sounds, you can see a pattern of where each particular allophone occurs:

lan 'a kind of flower'   *nara* 'if'
lika 'science'   *amari* 'extra'
lusu 'absence'   *sore* 'that'
lekishi 'history'   *naru* 'to ring'
loku 'six'   *iro* 'color'

You will see that [l] only occurs at the beginning of a word, never in the middle; [ɾ] occurs in the middle of a word, and never at the beginning.

In English the two sounds divide up into phonemes like this:

71

PHONOLOGY 2

```
l ———— [l]
r ———— [ɹ]
```

In Japanese they divide up into phonemes like this:

Allophonic variation like this can be expressed as rules (really principles). If you look again at the Japanese set of words above, you can see that [l] and [ɾ] are allophones of a single phoneme (there are no minimal pairs), and each sound only occurs in a specific environment - they are in complementary distribution, or don't occur in the same places.

Now let's look at some similar data (a set of words) from Korean. Let's look at the sounds [l] and [ɾ] in this data. Do they contrast or are they in complementary distribution? If they are in complementary distribution, we need to write a rule describing the complementary distribution.

1	[kal]	that'll go	12	[kɨrem]	then
2	[silkwa]	fruit	13	[tatɨl]	all of them
3	[kɨnɨl]	shade	14	[kəɾiɾo]	to the street
4	[tɨlcʰaŋ]	window	15	[ilkop]	seven
5	[mul]	water	16	[saɾam]	person
6	[əlmana]	how much	17	[ipalsa]	barber
7	[pal]	leg	18	[uɾi]	we
8	[iɾumi]	name	19	[onɨlppam]	tonight
9	[pʰal]	arm	20	[jəɾɨm]	summer
10	[kiɾi]	road	21	[pulpʰjən]	discomfort
11	[səul]	Seoul			

If we check the data first for minimal pairs, we don't find any. So, that means we don't have a contrast in the sounds. Remember that if there are minimal pairs, that means the sounds distinguish meaning and are separate phonemes. These two sounds then, are not separate phonemes. (Note: this is just an example, so the data is limited. If you were doing actual phonological analysis in a language, you would work with the whole language as a resource, not a restricted amount of data like this.)

Seeing we didn't find minimal pairs, we should now look for complementary environments. If we look at each word in the data, we can see that it doesn't matter what comes before these two sounds – both always follow vowels. What does matter is what comes *after* the sounds – if there is a vowel after it, this phoneme has the allophone [ɾ], but if there is a consonant after it, or if it is at the end of a word (i.e. there is nothing after it), it has the allophone [l]. We have found a pattern in the way the sounds work together - complementary distribution. We can express this complementary distribution by a rule:

/l/ → [ɾ] / _ V
    → [l] / elsewhere

Phonological rules like this are written in a specific way. On the left is the phoneme /l/ in slashes. Slashes are used to go around phonemes. The arrows mean 'becomes', or 'turns into' or 'is pronounced as'. Then the two allophones, [ɾ] and [l] are in square brackets. Square brackets are used for phones (speech sounds). In phonology they are used for allophones, because allophones are just ways of pronouncing a phoneme. Then there is a slash, and what follows each slash is the *environment* for that allophone. The first environment is _V. The line shows where the sound goes. V means 'vowel'. So that environment means 'when the sound appears before a vowel'. The second environment is 'elsewhere'. This means that this allophone occurs in a few different other environments – anywhere except the specific environment where you get [ɾ] (before a vowel).

Some other ways to write different environments are:

_ C (when the sound appears before a consonant)

_ # (This symbol in these rules means 'word boundary'. So this means 'when the sound appears before a word boundary' - at the end of a word).

You might wonder, for the rule we wrote for [l] and [ɾ] in Korean, why we didn't list both the environments where [l] occurs rather than just saying 'elsewhere'. Something like:

→ [l] / _ C
→ [l] / _ #

We don't list both of these because they have nothing in common. There is nothing specific about these environments that causes this allophone to occur in those places, it is just simply what you get when that phoneme is anywhere else than before a vowel. The rule we did list is specific - there is something about that environment that means it is where you will *always* get [ɾ]. Whenever there are a few unrelated environments that we can't generalize about, like where the [l] occurs, we simply say the environment for it is 'elsewhere'.

PHONOLOGY 2

Why is phonetics and phonology important?

Let's take a step back and look at the big picture of why it might be helpful for us to understand language on this level. It is probably obvious to you that in developing a writing system for a language, phonology is important - we need to know which sounds in a language are phonemically significant because those will need a separate symbol in the orthography (writing system) for people to be able to read their language. But an understanding of the principles of phonetics and phonology will also help to give you insight when you are learning to communicate in another language as well.

Have you ever had the experience of trying to say a word or name in another language, and no matter how many times you repeat it (you think correctly), your friend repeats it back to you and makes you say it again and again - because you are just not saying it *right*? But you can't hear any difference between how he is saying it and how you are saying it.

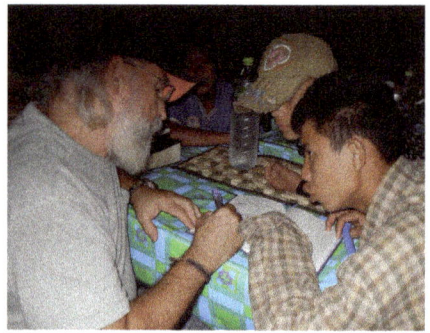

What might be happening is that the sound you are messing up in his language is not phonemically distinct in English. In other words, it may be a sound that can be said in a variety of ways in English, and it makes no difference to meaning (an allophone of one phoneme) so you don't even notice it. But in his language, these same variations may be separate phonemes - so switching them actually changes the meaning. Your friend feels it is important for you to get it just right when you pronounce it - to make sure the aspiration is there, or the nasalisation, or the lengthening - because to him the sound you are saying is actually an entirely different sound which indicates a different meaning. To him it would sound like someone trying to say the English word *worse* and saying *verse* instead - or saying *ship* instead of *sheep*. So, it is important for you to understand that it isn't just the sounds that are different in another language, but there will be differences in the way the language uses sounds to convey meaning.

Procedure for phonological analysis

We have covered phonology in a simplified way, because it actually gets quite complicated in practice. There are many different possible features of sounds (like voicing, lengthening, nasalisation) that can potentially change phonemes in different environments. Our purpose in this course is to give you a basic idea of the way sounds work differently in different languages and to have a basic understanding of the procedure for phonological analysis - not to be a trained analyst. If you are required in the future to do phonological analysis on a language, you will need to do further study on the full procedure and there are many helpful resources available. Also, you can often find help from others (linguists) who have been, or are working in that language or a related language or dialect.

To give you an idea of what the procedure looks like in practice, we will look at two examples involving vowel length - one example is more complex than the other. When you read these examples, don't worry if you don't understand everything. It will give you an idea of the *types* of things that can be encountered in phonological analysis and how the process looks.

Vowel Length in Kikuyu

In Kikuyu, vowels can either be pronounced as 'long' (in duration) or 'short' (in duration).

In IPA, a 'long' vowel is written with a colon following it.

    [kera] 'cross over'   [ke:ra] 'realise'

    [daka] 'beautiful'   [da:ka] 'play'

    [kua] 'die'   [ku:a] 'carry'

    [dura] 'spit'   [du:ra] 'stay'

    [kora] 'find'   [ko:ra] 'little frog'

Question: In Kikuyu, are the long vowels and short vowels allophones of the same, or different phonemes?

Our first step is to determine if there are minimal pairs for the long vowels and the short vowels. There are! So we stop. We can conclude that in Kikuyu, long vowels and short vowels are allophones of different phonemes.

Vowel Length in English

In English, vowels are also pronounced as either 'long' or 'short'.

    'ride' [ɹa:jd]   'right' [ɹajt]   'rye' [ɹaj]

    'aid' [e:jd]   'ate' [ejt]   'bay' [bej]

    'lobe' [lo:wb]   'lope' [lowp]   'low' [low]

    'teethe' [thi:ð]   'teeth' [thiθ]   'tea' [thi]

    'save' [se:jv]   'safe' [sejf]   'say' [sej]

Question: In English, are the long vowels and short vowels allophones of the same, or different phonemes?

PHONOLOGY 2

First, we need to determine if there are minimal pairs for the long vowels and the short vowels. It turns out that there are not any minimal pairs for any short and long vowels. So, we go on to determine if there is a phonological rule that can relate the long and short vowels to the same phoneme.

OK, now how do we find out if there is such a rule? The process is not 'cut-and-dried', but, it can be broken down into four sub-steps. Our search is actually logical, and if we follow the steps we will get to the correct answer. We want to determine which of the following statements is true:

1. There's a rule that requires long vowels to be pronounced as short in some environment.

    OR

2. There's a rule that requires short vowels to be pronounced as long in some environment.

Some reasoning:

If (1) were true, then...there would be some environment where we only find short vowels (and no long vowels).

If (2) were true, then...there would be some environment where we only find long vowels (and no short vowels).

An Analogy

Suppose there are two kinds of creatures:

- The brown octopus, that sometimes turns blue.
- The blue octopus, that sometimes turns brown.

How could we tell if we had a brown octopus or a blue octopus?

We could watch it for a while, and see whether:

- There is some particular occasion when it becomes blue (e.g. when it is alarmed), or
- There is some particular occasion when it becomes brown (e.g. when it is defending itself).

If there is some occasion when it's always blue... then it's actually a brown octopus, but there is some rule that turns it into a blue octopus sometimes.

If there is some occasion when it's always brown... then it's actually a blue octopus, but there is some rule that turns it brown in particular circumstances.

TUTORIAL 5.9

So, getting back to our problem of long and short vowels in English - we want to see which of these is true:

There is some environment where you *only* find short vowels.

If so, then there is a rule which turns long vowels into short vowels there.

OR

There is some environment where you *only* find long vowels.

If so, then there is a rule which turns short vowels into long vowels there.

We are going to figure out which of these is true by following four steps:

Step 1:

Determine the *environments* of the two phones (short vowels and long vowels). We want to make up four lists:
- The phones that precede a long vowel
- The phones that follow a long vowel
- The phones that precede a short vowel
- The phones that follow a short vowel

'ride' [ɹaːjd]	'right' [ɹajt]	'rye' [ɹaj]
'aid' [eːjd]	'ate' [ejt]	'bay' [bej]
'lobe' [loːwb]	'lope' [lowp]	'low' [low]
'teethe' [thiːð]	'teeth' [thiθ]	'tea' [thi]
'save' [seːjv]	'safe' [sejf]	'say' [sej]

The phones that precede a long vowel are: [ɹ] # [l] [th] [s]

The phones that follow a long vowel are: [d] [b] [ð] [v] [j] [w]

The phones that precede a short vowel are: [ɹ] # [l] [th] [s] [b]

The phones that follow a short vowel are: [t] [p] [θ] [f] # [j] [w]

Step 2:

For each environment, look for any *commonalities* between the sounds in question. We want to make up four lists:
- Similarities between the phones that precede a long vowel
- Similarities between the phones that follow a long vowel
- Similarities between the phones that precede a short vowel
- Similarities between the phones that follow a short vowel

NOTE: No phones share anything in common with '#'.

The phones that precede a long vowel: [ɹ] [l] [th] [s] - **Nothing in common**
The phones that follow a long vowel: [d] [b] [ð] [v] [j] [w] - **All are voiced!**
The phones that precede a short vowel: [ɹ] [l] [th] [s] [b] - **Nothing in common**
The phones that follow a short vowel: [t] [p] [θ] [f] [j] [w] - **Nothing in common**

Step 3:
See if any of the *environments are unique* to a particular allophone. For each phone (long vowel or short vowel)...look at those environments for [X] where the sounds share something in common...check whether the corresponding environment for [Y] can have those properties...if not, then that environment is *unique to* [X]!

See if any environments are unique to a particular allophone:

The phones that precede a long vowel: [ɹ] # [l] [th] [s] - **Nothing in common**
The phones that follow a long vowel: [d] [b] [ð] [v] [j] [w] - **All are voiced!**
The phones that precede a short vowel: [ɹ] # [l] [th] [s] [b] - **None in common**
The phones that follow a short vowel: [t] [p] [θ] [f] # [j] [w] - **None in common**

Now look at the corresponding environments for the other phone. See if they can share those properties too.

The phones that follow a long vowel: [d] [b] [ð] [v] [j] [w] - **All are voiced!**
The phones that follow a short vowel: [t] [p] [θ] [f] # [j] [w] - **None in common**

Only long vowels can precede voiced Consonants!

Step 4:
If there is an environment unique to one phone, write out the rule that would limit that phone to that environment. Remember our logic from earlier:

- If there is some environment where you only find short vowels...then there is a rule that turns long vowels into short vowels there.
- If there is some environment where you only find long vowels...then there is a rule that turns short vowels into long vowels there.

Rule of Thumb:
If there are two allophones [X] and [Y], and only [X] appears in environment Z, the rule is*: "/Y/ is pronounced as [X] in Z".*

Our Question: In English, are the long vowels and short vowels allophones of the same or different phonemes?

The Answer:
They are allophones of the same phoneme (namely, short vowels).
The phonological rule that relates them is the following:
"In English, a short vowel is pronounced as a long vowel when preceding a voiced consonant."

$$/V/ \rightarrow [V:] / \_\text{Voiced-C}$$

"A short V is pronounced as a long V when preceding a voiced C"

Summary of the procedure

Suppose you want to determine whether two phones ([X] and [Y]) in some language are allophones of the same (or different) phonemes. If there are not minimal pairs for [X] and [Y], determine if there is a phonological rule that can relate [X] and [Y] to the same phoneme.

Step 1:
Determine the environments of the two phones.

Step 2:
For each environment, look for any commonalities between the sounds in question.

Step 3:
See if any environments are unique to a particular allophone.

Step 4:
If there is an environment unique to one phone, write out the rule that would limit that phone to that environment.

PHONOLOGY 2

➡ ACTIVITIES

1. Take note of any long vowels in English that you read or hear in conversations. Confirm that they are always followed by voiced consonants. Another way to express this phonological rule of English (that only long vowels can precede voiced consonants) would be to say that *native speakers usually lengthen the vowel before voiced consonants*. Try the exercise below to see this phenomenon working. Read each pair of words out loud. The second word in each pair has a voiced consonant after the vowel, so as a native speaker of English, you will naturally lengthen the vowel sound before it.

branch / flange, march / charge, pinch / binge,

leaf / leave, moat / mowed, wrote / road

2. Use the four steps in the procedure we learned above to determine whether the two phones in each language below are allophones of the same (or different) phonemes. Write the phonological rule for each one. (answers on the next page).

Sierra Nahuat (Mexico)

- compare [t] and [tʰ]
    [tetʰ] *stone*
    [tagol] *corn*
    [kitoka] *he chases it*
    [tʃonti] *hair*
    [epatʰ] *skunk*
    [sinitʰ] *leaf*

Agarabi (PNG)

- compare **[p]** and **[f]**
    [pane] *hornbill*
    [pon] *pig*
    [tohpe] *knife*
    [wompon] *design*
    [warufah] *village*
    [yafo] *fill*
    [anafin] *in the bamboo*

Mianmin (PNG)

- compare **[k]** and **[kh]**
    [uktem] *ask*
    [kwam] *club*
    [skʰilon] *foot*
    [kʰakʰet] *finger*
    [neekʰ] *friend*
    [kweŋ] *insect*
    [biksa] *picture*

 ANSWER

Sierra Nahuat (Mexico)
- compare [t] and [tʰ]
    [th] / _ # (is word final) / [t] elsewhere.

Agarabi (PNG)
- compare [p] and [f]
    /p/ → [f] / V_V
    [p] becomes [f] when it is between two vowels.

Mianmin (PNG)
- compare [k] and [kʰ]
    /kʰ/ → [k] / _ C
    [kʰ] becomes [k] when it precedes a consonant.

5.10 Morphology 1

OBJECTIVES OF THIS TUTORIAL

This tutorial introduces the study of morphemes, the internal structure of words, and the rules by which words are formed. This is called morphology.

Introduction

Words are the smallest independent meaningful units in language. But words can be divided into even smaller meaningful pieces. These smaller meaningful units are called *morphemes*.

Words have an internal structure of one or more morphemes. For example, *pigs* has an internal structure of two morphemes:

pig, a noun,

-s, a morpheme meaning 'more than one'.

The word *undesirability* has an internal structure of four morphemes:

desire, a verb,

un-, a morpheme meaning 'not',

-able, a morpheme meaning 'able to be',

-ity, a morpheme meaning something like 'the idea of'.

The morpheme is the minimal combination of sound and meaning which cannot be further divided. The study of morphemes, the internal structure of words, and the rules by which words are formed is called *morphology*. Traditionally this is referred to as 'word formation'.

We say that words that consist of just one morpheme are *monomorphemic*. Words that consist of more than one morpheme are *polymorphemic*.

Free and Bound morphemes

Some morphemes can be words on their own (e.g. **cat**, **desire**). These are called *free* morphemes. Some morphemes can't occur by themselves. They can only occur when they are attached to another morpheme (e.g. **-s**, **un-**, **-able**, **-ity**). These are called *bound* morphemes.

So in **cats** there are two morphemes: **cat**, which is free, and **-s**, which is bound.

The part of a word that is a free morpheme is in a sense the core of the word, to which the bound morphemes attach. Usually it carries the central meaning of the word. This is called the word *root*. Sometimes word roots are bound morphemes, but most often they are free.

Affixes

Most bound morphemes are *affixes* - we call them that because they are affixed or attached to the root of a word.

Morphemes can't just be put together in any order. Some affixes have to go before the root and some after it, for example:

cat-s (not **s-cat**)

un-desir-able (not **desir-able-un**)

The morpheme **un-** has to go *before* the root. An affix that has to go before the root is called a *prefix*. Other affixes have to follow the root, like the **-s** in *cats*. An affix that has to follow the root is called a *suffix*.

So, in a word like *mistrustful* we have two bound morphemes, the prefix **mis-** and the suffix **-ful**, surrounding the root, **trust**, so we get **mis-trust-ful**. Or in a word like **friendliness**, we have a root followed by two suffixes: **friend-li-ness**.

In any language with affixes there are also rules about what *order* the suffixes and prefixes occur in. For example:

We can add the suffix **-ly** to the root **right** and get **rightly**.

Or we could add the suffix **-ful** and get **rightful**.

We can also add both suffixes, and get **rightfully**, but they have to be in that order, the reverse order is not possible: (**rightlyful**).

In some languages, there are a few other types of morphemes. One is the *infix*. Infixes are placed inside the root, rather than before or after it. For example, in Tagalog there is an infix (**-in-**) that is inserted after the first consonant of a root verb:

sulat 'write' → s-in-ulat 'was written'

Another type of morpheme is the *circumfix*. A circumfix goes on both sides of a root – one part goes before it, and one goes after it. It's a bit like a prefix and a suffix at the same time, but they have to both be attached together. For example, in German the past tense is formed using the circumfix (**ge- -t**):

machen 'to make' → **ge-mach-t** 'made'

Compounding

Another way that words are formed is *compounding*. Instead of adding affixes to a root, it joins two separate roots to form a new word. English has the word **green** and the word **house**. We also have a compound word **greenhouse**, which is one word formed out of these two component words.

With compound words, the meanings are not entirely predictable from the roots that make up the compound. So a **green house** (two words) is a house which is green, while a **greenhouse** (one word) is a special kind of building for growing plants in. The building is not a house in the normal sense, and the building itself is not green. The compound word has quite a different meaning to the original words that make it up. In English many compounds are written as one word, like **greenhouse**, while others are written with a hyphen, as in **icy-cold**, or are even written as if it was two words, like **light year**. These are all still *compounds* though.

Other ways of forming words

Compounding is just one way that new words are formed. Here are a few more:

- An **acronym** is formed out of the first letter of each word of a phrase. It's not uncommon to hear someone *lol* at a good joke (from LOL — laugh out loud). *Scuba* (S̲elf-C̲ontained U̲nderwater B̲reathing A̲pparatus) and *radar* (R̲A̲dio D̲etection A̲nd R̲anging) are examples of older acronyms that we don't necessarily recognise as such anymore.

- A **backformation** removes a part of the word that resembles a morpheme in order to coin a new word. For example, in the word *burglar*, English speakers misanalysed the *-r* as a suffix, similar to the *-r* in *writer*. They wanted to create a verb meaning 'steal', so they removed the *-r* and we ended up with the verb *burgle*. The International Airport in Milwaukee has a lounge area just beyond security called the *recombobulation area* — formed by backformation from the word *discombobulate* where the *dis-* was mistakenly taken to be a prefix and then replaced with the common prefix *re-*. The "recombobulation area" is a place where you can get yourself organised: put your shoes back on, put your laptop back into your bag, etc.

- A **blend** combines two words to create a new word. *Smog* is a blend of *smoke* plus

fog. *Mockumentary* combines *mock* and *documentary*. *Jeggings* are snug-fitting *leggings* that look like *jeans*.
- **Clipping** is the reduction of a word into one of its component parts. The recently coined word *app* meaning 'application for a mobile device' was clipped from *application*.

Examples such as these illustrate the creative capacity of language. It is our knowledge of *morphology* - the rules of how we can combine the smallest meaningful units in language - that allows us to combine the pieces of old words to create something new.

How morphemes work
Different morphemes have different functions - they *do* different things. Look at the following English words:

>   walk, walked, walker

When the morpheme -**ed** is added to *walk*, it creates a different form of the same word. But when the morpheme -**er** is added to *walk*, it creates a whole new word with a new meaning. This is because the morphemes -**ed** and -**er** are different kinds of suffixes: we say that -**ed** is an *inflectional* suffix, while -**er** is a *derivational* suffix. We will explain *derivation* and *inflection* below.

Derivation
Derivation changes the *meaning* of words. Derivational morphemes create a new word with a new meaning. In the examples below, the derivational morphemes **un-** and **re-** are added:

>   true → untrue
>
>   paint → repaint

Notice that in both of these cases the meaning of the word changes - *untrue* means the opposite of *true*, and *repaint* means to *paint*, but specifically to do it again.

In these examples, although the meaning changes, the *type* of word (word class) stays the same. *True* and *untrue* are both adjectives, and *paint* and *repaint* are both verbs. The important thing is that derivation always changes *meaning*.

As well as changing meaning, derivation *can* also change the type of word (word class). We saw that in our first example - *walk* is a verb, referring to an action. *Walker* is a noun referring to a kind of person. You can see this in these examples:

> write → writ-er
>
> slow → slow-ly
>
> sleep → sleep-y → sleep-i-ness.

In English, morphemes that change word class are usually suffixes. But there are some exceptions, like **en-** (**en-rage, en-circle**).

In other languages morphemes that change word class are usually prefixes. For example, in Fijian **vaka-** which means 'in the manner of'. It turns an adjective or noun into an adverb:

> **totolo** 'fast' → **vaka-totolo** 'quickly'
>
> **marama** 'lady' → **vaka-marama** 'in a ladylike way'

Inflection

Inflection creates a *different form* of the same word, with the same basic meaning. It affects the way a word relates to other words in the grammar of the language. So, while derivation adds meaning, inflection adds grammatical information.

Inflection can't change word class. For example, the suffix **-s** on English verbs, as in **he shows**. The event is exactly the same as the event in *I show* or *you show*. The action performed is exactly the same. The difference between *show* and *shows* is that with *shows* the action has to be done by *he, she* or *it* (it must have a third person singular subject), while *show* can't. So this suffix interacts with other grammatical features of the sentence - it makes the sentence work according to the grammatical rules - but it doesn't change the meaning of the word.

Some other examples of inflectional morphemes are:

The ending **-ed** adds grammatical information (*tense*) -

> he showed me the paper

The ending **-ing** adds grammatical information (*aspect* - basically that the event is ongoing):

> he was showing me the paper

The endings **-ed /-en /-n** add grammatical information (*aspect* - that the event is completed):

> he has shown me the paper

Show, shows, showed, showing and *shown* are not different words with different meanings, they are different forms of the same word – the verb 'to show'.

Some examples of inflectional morphemes on other types of word classes in English are:

MORPHOLOGY 1

Nouns: a cat → two cats
           book → books
Verbs: -s   John read-s books
           -ing   They are work-ing
           -ed   They work-ed
           -en   They have eat-en
Adjectives: -er   the small-er one
               -est the small-est one

Children learning English, as well as adult second language learners, have a strong tendency to make irregular forms regular, making amusing errors such as *goed* for *went*, or *foots* for *feet*. These errors show that what's being learned is a *rule*, something like our brain thinking "just add *–ed* to make the past tense", rather than having to learn past-tense verbs one at a time. The errors that children make show that children don't just imitate their parents - they assume that language has regular morphological rules. All languages *do* have morphological rules and we will be looking at some more examples of different languages in the next tutorial.

➡ ACTIVITIES

1. Find five new words that have entered the English language over the last 5 - 10 years. What word formation process did they rely on?

Do the following practice exercises (the answers are at the end, but try to do them on your own first).

2. Divide the following words into morphemes. (Example: *barefoot* - morphemes: bare-foot)

   a. research
   b. butterfly
   c. holiday
   d. plants
   e. blackboard
   f. living
   g. wording

3. Some of the words in this list contain suffixes. Identify the suffixes by underlining them.

a. happiness
b. unkind
c. freedom
d. flowers
e. loneliness
f. blackboard

4. Some of the words in this list contain prefixes. Identify the prefixes by underlining them.

a. unable
b. discourage
c. establish
d. receive
e. strawberry
f. amoral

5. Identify the root in the words in this list by underlining it. (Example: friendly)

a. lamps
b. kindness
c. hinted
d. players
e. editors
f. grandfathers

6. For each of the following bound morphemes, determine whether it is derivational or inflectional and give two words in which it appears. Remember some can be both derivational and inflectional, if so, give examples of the suffix being used both ways. (Example: –able: derivational. *eatable*; *readable*)

a. –ity
b. –s
c. un–
d. –ing
e. –er
f. –ed

7. From the following list of words, select **four** words with inflectional morphology and then select **four** words with derivational morphology.

MORPHOLOGY 1

elements	have	killed
gain	linked	such
and	Indo-European	cram
unkind	speech	tend
as	egg	the
some	off	these
case	ordering	thought
example	one	within
feature	morphology	great

2.
   a. re-search

ANSWER

   b. butter-fly
   c. holi-day (the root word is *holy*)
   d. plant-s
   e. black-board
   f. liv-ing (the root word is *live*)
   g. word-ing

3.
   a. happiness
   b. unkind (no suffix, -un is a prefix and *kind* is the root)
   c. freedom
   d. flowers
   e. loneli-ness (two suffixes)
   f. blackboard (no suffix, this is a compound)

4.
   a. unable
   b. discourage
   c. establish
   d. receive (based on Latin *recipere*, from *re-* 'back' + *capere* 'take.')
   e. strawberry (no prefix, this is a compound)
   f. amoral

5.
   a. lamps
   b. kindness
   c. hinted
   d. players
   e. editors
   f. grandfathers

6.
   a. -ity: derivational (stupid → stupidity, fluid → fluidity)
   b. -s: inflectional (smells, dogs)
   c. un-: derivational (wise → unwise, kind → unkind)
   d. -ing: inflectional (working, eating) and derivational (build → building, nourish → nourishing)
   e. -er: inflectional (smaller, nicer) and derivational (work → worker, write → writer)
   f. -ed: inflectional (sorted, minced)

MORPHOLOGY 1

inflectional (grammatical) e.g. -ed, -'s, -s, -er, -ed, -es, -est and -ing
(if it is used to turn a verb into e.g. present participle - example: break → breaking, eat → eating)

derivational (lexical - changes meaning): words formed by the attachment of derivational affixes are *derived* from other words, but have a different meaning, e.g. **dis-, re-, in-, be-, en-, -ly, -ance, -able, -ize, -ish, -like, -ment** and **-ing** (if it is used to turn the verb into a noun: example: build → a building, two buildings, nourish → nourishing)

7.

Inflectional: elements, linked, ordering, killed

Derivational: unkind, Indo-European, morphology, within

5.11 Morphology 2

OBJECTIVES OF THIS TUTORIAL

This tutorial explains some more aspects of morphology, and looks at some examples from different languages.

Introduction
We noted in the last tutorial that in every language, there are rules of how morphemes fit together to form words - they must be in a certain order and in a certain place in the word. We also looked at some different types of morphemes and what function those different types have.

Stems and Roots
The *root* of a word, as we said before, is most often a free morpheme (it can stand on its own) to which the bound morphemes attach. It carries the central meaning of the word and could be thought of as the core of the word.

Derivational affixes (that change the meaning) are normally closer to the root than inflectional morphemes (that carry grammatical information).

    So we say **walk-er-s** (not **walk-s-er**)

So the information (derivational affix) that changes the meaning of the word comes before the information (inflectional affix) that adds grammatical information (in this case, makes it a plural).

We say that derivational suffixes attach to *roots* to create *stems*. The stem in the word above is *walker*. A stem is a word in its own right. Inflectional affixes are added to stems, not roots. The meaning must be established first and then the grammatical information is added to that.

Morphology and the Lexicon
The final question we need to consider about morphemes is a fairly basic one: how are they stored? Speakers of a language store morphemes in a *lexicon* - a mental dictionary that they have in their minds.

MORPHOLOGY 2

There are two main differences between the mental lexicon and an ordinary (written) dictionary:

- The mental lexicon does not contain words that have more than one morpheme in them, whereas dictionaries include complex words.
- The lexicon people store in their minds contains bound morphemes, whereas dictionaries don't usually contain entries for bound morphemes.

Let's explain that a bit more. Speaking is a *creative* process - we are able to take a limited number of pieces of language and combine them using specific rules to create an unlimited number of utterances. We don't have to *memorise* every single thing we are ever going to say. We have a certain number pieces (free and bound morphemes) stored in our lexicon, and we are able to combine them according to grammatical rules to say what we want to say.

So, when we want to *write* a lexicon for a language, we want to follow the same logical pattern that people use to store morphemes in their mental lexicon. We follow the pattern of writing just the pieces - the separate morphemes - and we don't write every single word that can be made by combining those morphemes.

We write these morphemes as *lexical entries*. A lexical entry includes many pieces of information, including a meaning; the group of sounds that convey that meaning; the lexical category, etc. For example:

    walk   V root 'bipedal locomotion characteristic of humans'

Walk is a verb (V), it is a root, and it means a certain action.

But what about a word like *walking*, which consists of two morphemes?

We do not store the whole word in the lexicon - like this:

    walking   V 'bipedal locomotion characteristic of humans; progressive aspect'

The problem with this kind of listing is that you end up with lots of words that mean much the same thing. This is a problem in English, but it gets to be a much bigger problem in languages with really complex morphology. You would end up with thousands of related forms.

So we avoid listing *walk*, *walks*, *walking* and *walked* as separate lexical entries. We don't give every word a lexical entry, but we give every *morpheme* its own lexical entry.

So as well as lexical entries like the one for *walk* above, there'll also be lexical entries of the following type for bound morphemes.

    -ing   TA 'Progressive aspect'

-ed	TA 'Past tense'
-s	NUM 'Plural'
-ly	ADV 'Manner'
re-	'Do again'

These lexical entries have basically the same form as the lexical entry for the free morpheme **walk**. They contain a meaning and the sounds that conveys that meaning.

The only difference from the entry for the free morpheme is that they contain a hyphen indicating where they attach to. So for a suffix, like -ing, the hyphen comes before the sound because -ing attaches to the end of the verb. For a prefix, like **re-**, the hyphen comes after the sound because **re-** attaches to the beginning of the verb.

Notice that -ed and -ing both have the lexical category TA. This means "tense or aspect". We give this that lexical category because -ed indicates tense (past tense), while -ing indicates aspect (progressive aspect, i.e. the event is ongoing), but these two fit into the same position in a word. We can say *walked* or *walking*.

The plural marker has the lexical category NUM, meaning "number". The suffix –ly has the lexical category ADV, because it has the effect of turning an adjective into an adverb – it brings its own lexical category to the word it builds. But **re-** doesn't have a lexical category at all because it has no effect on word class – it attaches to verbs and they stay verbs. Don't worry too much if some of these terms are new to you, we will be explaining them in more detail later when we look at the structure of English.

Allomorphy

Sometimes morphemes can have different phonological forms - and change their sound depending on their environment. Just as we saw that a phoneme can have different allophones in different environments, a morpheme can also have different *allomorphs* in different environments. For example, in English the morpheme for the indefinite article can be *a* or *an*:

a car, *a* house, and *a* piano,

an apple, *an* elephant, and *an* umbrella.

Whether we get *a* or *an* depends on the first sound in the word that comes after it. If that word begins with a consonant we get the allomorph *a*. If it begins with a vowel, we get the allomorph *an*.

Another example is the English regular past tense suffix -ed that attaches to verbs. This

MORPHOLOGY 2

morpheme actually has three forms: /-d/, /-t/ and /-əd/.

beg → *begged* /beg-d/
rob → *robbed* /ɹɒb-d/
hug → *hugged* /hʌg-d/
walk → *walked* /woːk-t/
nip → *nipped* /nɪp-t/
lock → *locked* /lɔk-t/
kiss → *kissed* /kɪs-t/

If the suffix comes after a voiced consonant you get /-d/ (which is voiced). If the suffix comes after a voiceless consonant you get /-t/ (which is voiceless). What if the suffix -ed comes after a vowel?

glue → *glued* /glʉ-d/
sigh → *sighed* /sɑe-d/
roar → *roared* /ɹoː-d/
sew → *sewed* /səʉ-d/

If the suffix comes after a vowel you get /-d/. Why? Because vowels are voiced. But that's not the end of the story.

need → *needed* /niːd-əd/
hoot → *hooted* /hʉt-əd/

If the suffix comes after /t/ or /d/, the suffix is /əd/. Why? Because the consonant at the end of the root is too similar to the consonant of the suffix – they're both alveolar plosives. They need to be separated by a vowel, so the most neutral vowel, schwa, is inserted to keep the consonant of the suffix separate from the consonant of the root.

This is a process called *assimilation* – something changes to become more like the sounds around it in some way. This is just one of the morphological rules that apply to our language and that we store in our minds as English speakers. Every language has different rules.

Differences in languages

It is in their morphology that we most clearly see the differences between languages. Some of the major types of morphologies are:

- **Isolating** - such as Chinese, Indonesian, Thai and Yoruba (West Africa). Isolating languages use grammatical morphemes that are separate words.
- **Agglutinating** - such as Turkish, Finnish, Tamil, Austronesian and Tibeto-Burman languages. Agglutinating languages use grammatical morphemes in the form of attached syllables called affixes.
- **Inflectional** - such as Russian, Latin and Arabic. Inflectional languages may go one step further and actually change the word at the phonemic level to express grammatical morphemes.

All languages are really mixed systems - it's all a matter of proportion. English, for example, uses all three methods.

Turkish is an example of an agglutinating language that makes extensive use of suffixes. One example is the Turkish word *terbiyesizliklerindenmis*:

'good manners'	*terbiye*
'without good manners, rude'	*terbiye**siz***
'rudeness'	*terbiyesiz**lik***
'their rudeness'	*terbiyesizlik**leri***
'from their rudeness'	*terbiyesizlikleri**nden***
'I gather that it was from their rudeness'	*terbiyesizliklerinden**mis***

 ACTIVITIES

Do the following exercises. Answers are provided below, but try to work them out for yourself first.

1. Divide the following words into their morphemes. Indicate which morphemes are inflectional and which are derivational.

    a. mistreatment
    b. deactivation

MORPHOLOGY 2

    c. psychology
    d. airsickness
    e. terrorized
    f. uncivilized
    g. lukewarm

3. Look at the following language data from Ata (PNG), then try to answer the questions. (The language is written in the Ata orthography, using the symbol ' for the glottal stop.)

a'a ulai no xai	'the dog will go to the garden'
a'a mulai no tuala	'the dog went to the village'
meme ulai no xai	'the pig will go to the garden'
tameme milai no xai	'the pigs went to the garden'
taa'a milai no lexa	'the dogs went to the river'
molomolo mulai no tuala	'the child went to the village'
tamolomolo milai no xai	'the children went to the garden'
meme ulai no tuala	'the pig will go to the village'
tamolomolo milai no tuala	'the children went to the village'
tamolomolo ilai no lexa	'the children will go to the river'

What are the Ata morphemes (roots) for 'garden', 'river', 'village', 'pig', 'dog', 'child'?

    a. How is the plural indicated morphemically?
    b. How is past tense indicated?
    c. Translate the following into Ata:
- 'the dog will go to the river'
- 'the child went to the river'
- 'the pigs went to the village'

    d. If the Ata root for man is '*mulu*', translate 'the man went to the river'.

 **ANSWER**

2. Words into their morphemes
  a. mistreatment = **treat** (root) + **mis-** (derivational) + **-ment** (derivational)
  b. deactivation = **act** (root) + **de-** (derivational) + **-ive** (derivational) + **-ate** (derivational) + **-ion** (derivational)
  c. psychology = **psych-** *or* **psyche** (root) + **-ology** (derivational)
  d. airsickness = **sick** (root) + **air** (derivational) + **-ness** (derivational)
  e. terrorised = **terror** (root) + **-ise** (derivational) + PAST (inflectional) if the word is a verb form
   OR terrorised = **terror** (root) + **-ise** (derivational) + **-ed** (derivational) if the word is an adjective
  f. uncivilised = **civ-** (root) + **-il** (derivational) + **un-** (derivational) + **-ise** (derivational) + **-ed** (derivational)
   The root is *"civ-"* because that root is also in words like *"civic."* In this case, the *"-ed"* must be derivational, because *"uncivilized"* cannot be a verb form.
  g. lukewarm = **lukewarm** (root) or: lukewarm = **warm** (root) + **luke** (derivational or root)

3. Ata Data:
  a. Ata morphemes: *xai* 'garden', *lexa* 'river', *tuala* 'village', *meme* 'pig', *a'a* 'dog', *molomolo* 'child'
  b. The plural is indicated by the *ta-* prefix on the noun (in Ata, this prefix is used for animate (living) things only - such as people and animals). The verb changes to indicate plural subjects also: *mu-* changes to *mi-* (past tense) and *u-* changes to *i-* (future/present tense). So plural subject with future/present tense would be *ilai* (they will go/ they are going), or with past tense it would be *milai* (they went).
  c. Past tense is morphemically indicated by the *m-* prefix on the verb (tense and aspect are actually much more complex in Ata, but from the data here, this is what you should have noticed). *m-* is prefixed on the verb to indicate past tense for singular subjects, changing from *ulai* to *mulai*, but with plural subjects the verb becomes *milai*.
  d. Translations:
   - a'a ulai no lexa *'the dog will go to the river'*
   - molomolo mulai no lexa *'the child went to the river'*
   - tameme milai no tuala *'the pigs went to the village'*
  e. mulu mulai no lexa *'the man went to the river'*

5.12 Syntax 1

> **OBJECTIVES OF THIS TUTORIAL**
>
> This tutorial and the next one introduce syntax - the unconscious principles people use to put words together into sentences. We will explain and describe what syntax is, and how to recognize and represent the ways that sentences are built, using examples from English and other languages.

Review English Grammar

It would be a great idea for you at this point - if you need to - to take some time to do a review of basic English grammar. Your goal would be to become familiar with the basic structure of English and the terminology used to describe it. This will give you a good foundation for the next tutorials which introduce the variety of possible structures that you may encounter in other languages. There are many resources for reviewing English grammar which are easy to use and that you might even find enjoyable, for example two free online resources are:

- *English Grammar 101*: http://englishgrammar101.com. A good resource for basic English grammar exercises, with online modules you can do as a review.
- *The Internet Grammar of English*: http://www.ucl.ac.uk/internet-grammar. An online course in English grammar written primarily for university undergraduates, with information and exercises on basic grammar. Also includes a good glossary of terms.

What is syntax?

Knowing a language doesn't just mean knowing all its sounds and words. It also means unconsciously knowing the principles for how words are put together to build sentences. These sets of unconscious principles are called the *syntax* of the language. If a speaker uses the correct rules for connecting words together, it is possible for them to create an infinite number of sentences, all of which are meaningful to a listener who also knows the same rules.

The rules of grammar do not have to be *explicitly* understood by the speaker of the language or the listener. The majority of native speakers of a language will have no formal knowledge of the grammar of language but are still capable of speaking the language grammatically to a great degree of accuracy. Native speakers of a language assimilate these rules subconsciously while the language is being learned as a child.

As we said before, the grammar of a language has several components:
- The *phonetics* that governs the structure of sounds;
- The *morphology* that governs the structure of words;
- The *syntax*, which governs the structure of sentences;
- The *semantics* that governs the meanings of words and sentences.

Since we have already investigated phonetics and morphology, now we are going to focus on syntax and later we will begin to look into semantics.

Phrase structure and argument structure

There are two main areas of syntax that overlap and are connected: phrase structure and argument structure.

The *phrase structure* of a language is the set of principles about how words are put together to make phrases, and how words and phrases are put together to build sentences. Phrase structure is also often called constituent structure, because it deals with the way the constituents (or separate parts) of a sentence are put together.

Argument structure is about the way the participants in an event are expressed in the grammar of a sentence (here, the term 'argument' doesn't mean a disagreement). In the sentence *Mary saw the dog*, the event has two participants (or arguments): Mary and the dog. One is the subject of the sentence, the other is the object. One is the participant who does the seeing, the other is the one who gets seen. The way a language tells us which is the subject and which is the object and so on, is called argument structure.

The syntax of a language is made up of the rules for phrase structure and the rules for argument structure.

An example of the phrase structure in English is the fact that most adjectives come before the noun they are telling us more about, e.g.: *the red house, the big dog, the yellow sun*. But other languages have a different phrase structure, for example in French most adjectives come after the noun: *la maison rouge* (the house red). This is also true for Ata (PNG): *tani lauoinu* (the house red).

Possible sentence structures

The main parts of a sentence are the subject (S), object (O) and verb (V). Different languages use different orders for these three parts in sentences. There are six possible orders: SVO, SOV, VSO, VOS, OSV and OVS, but most languages - over 80% - have the subject of the sentence first. Only a very small number have the object of the sentence first.

Also, over 90% of languages have the verb and object together. This makes sense, because the relationship between a verb and its object is particularly important. Why? Because if the verb and object are next to each other there can be a Verb Phrase, and every sentence must have a Noun Phrase and a Verb Phrase to make sense.

We are first going to look at some examples from English to show you how to diagram and discover how syntax works in your own language, then later we will take a look at some examples in other languages.

Phrases

Sentences are made up of smaller phrases. There are several different types of phrase that can be used in a sentence, but the two phrases which *must* be used in a sentence for it to make sense are a **noun phrase** and a **verb phrase**.

In a phrase, we *must* have a word which is called the **head**. This is the core of the phrase, what the phrase can't exist without. So in a phrase like 'the dog' or 'ran far away', in the first phrase 'dog' is the head because it is the main part of the phrase, and in the second phrase 'ran' is the head because it is essential for the phrase to exist. We can have 'dog ran', which isn't grammatical, but this still makes sense since we can understand that the dog ran. But we can't have 'the far away', this makes no sense to us!

Modifiers

So 'the' and 'far away' have to be given a name to distinguish them from the head. We call these **modifiers**. They modify the head and give it specific meaning. The **determiner** 'the' modifies the 'dog' because it lets us know which dog we are referring to. The phrase 'far away' modifies the verb 'ran' by letting us know the extent to which the dog ran.

Noun Phrases

A noun phrase is usually the person or thing that is performing the verb in the sentence. It may also be the person or thing that the verb is being done to in a sentence.

The person doing the verb in a sentence is known as the **subject**. For example, in the sentence 'Tom pushed the car', 'Tom' is the subject of the sentence as he is pushing the car. 'The car' is the object in the sentence as the car is the object that the verb is being done to. Both of these are noun phrases.

SYNTAX 1

A noun phrase has to contain a **noun**, such as a name or a tangible object. Sometimes, a determiner is also needed in a noun phrase, for example *'a cat'*, *'the* dog' - *'a'* and *'the'* are called determiners because they tell us which person or thing is involved in the sentence.

Syntax Trees

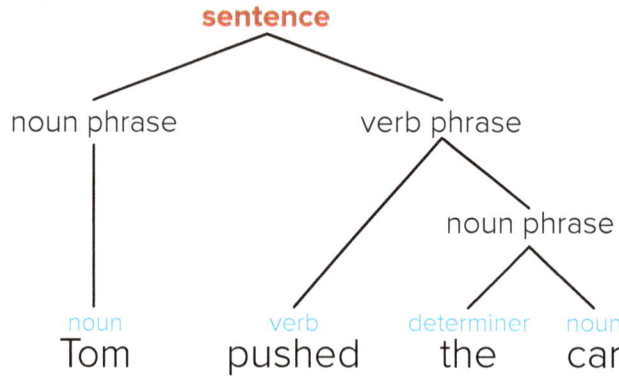

To explain sentence structures, we draw trees, like the one above. It is actually a lot more complicated than it looks, so we will explain it step by step. We start with the noun phrase, *the car*. We know a noun phrase is made up of a determiner and a noun. First, we label what parts of speech each of these are:

Next, we can draw two lines to join them together, creating a noun phrase:

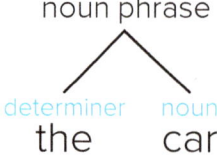

If we look at the proper noun, *Tom*, we find it is a little bit different. A proper noun does not need a determiner, so we can go straight to making it another noun phrase:

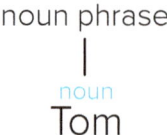

Now, we have drawn noun phrases for both 'Tom' and 'the car' in our sentence. But we aren't quite finished yet, now we need to talk about *verb phrases*.

TUTORIAL 5.12

Verb Phrases

Now that we have made some noun phrases, we can move on to verb phrases. The good news is a basic verb phrase can be made up of one word. The bad news is not every sentence has a basic verb phrase. For now let's look at the basic verb phrase and how the verb phrase fits in. First, we identify the verb and label its part of speech.

verb
pushed

Next, we can label it as a verb phrase. This is connected to the noun phrase 'the car', so we connect them and write the label above. But why is this the case?

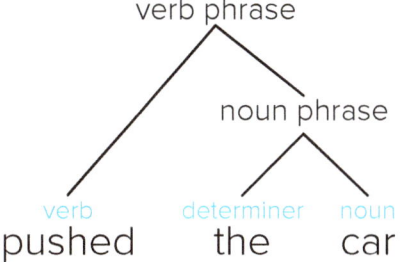

We need to link all of this together. In this sentence, we must join up all of the phrases to make a tree that says 'Sentence' at the top. But we can't just simply join up the lines, we need a structure! In order to figure out the correct structure, we need to look at constituents and how they are related to one another.

Constituents: words and phrases

In most languages, words can't just be put together in any order. For example, look at this sentence: *Last Tuesday the big fat cat chased the small ugly dog.*

You can understand the meaning of that sentence because of the way the words are grouped together into phrases - in the way that English grammar requires. But if it is written like this, it no longer makes any sense: *Small big chased Tuesday dog ugly fat the last cat the*

This second sentence is ungrammatical. For it to be grammatical, the words *the*, *big*, *fat* and *cat* have to group together in a particular way to form a particular kind of phrase.

Words are the most basic building blocks that are used to build sentences - they are the component parts, or *constituents*, of a sentence, and words can also group together into larger units called phrases. So, groups of words (phrases) are also *constituents*. Syntax uses *constituents* as building blocks, and constituents can either be words or phrases.

105

SYNTAX 1

Syntax does not have a flat structure where words just follow each other in a row. Words join with other words to form phrases, and they in turn join with other words and phrases to form bigger phrases, and so on. So syntax has a hierarchical, nested structure, where constituents combine with other constituents to form bigger constituents, which combine with other constituents to form even bigger constituents, right up to sentences. That is why it is helpful to draw syntax trees, because they represent this hierarchical structure.

In our example above, *big* and *fat* combine to form the phrase *big fat*, which then combines with *cat* to form the phrase *big fat cat*, which joins with *the* to form the phrase *the big fat cat*, which then combines with *chased* to form the phrase *the big fat cat chased*, etc.

To put it the other way around, constituents like sentences contain smaller constituents such as phrases, and these in turn contain even smaller constituents such as words and phrases, all the way down to each individual word.

Tests for constituency

So, what is a constituent? A constituent is a word or a group of words that function together as a unit. We can figure out fairly easily what words or groups of words are constituents by performing tests on them. There are four tests which can be used on any suspected constituent. These are:

1. *Omission* – Create the same sentence but take away the word/words we are testing.
2. *Replacement* – Can we replace the word/words with just a single word?
3. *Standalone* – Can we form a question using the sentence, and the answer be the word/words being tested?
4. *Movement* – Can we move the position of the word/words in the sentence and have the sentence still make sense without changing the meaning?

Let's do some examples of these tests so you can see how they work.

First, *omission*. If we take the sentence 'He sat down in the car', we can use the omission test to figure out the constituents in the sentence. Let's take 'in the car' as our constituent. If we take this away, does the sentence still make sense grammatically?

'He sat down in the car.'

'He sat down.'

The sentence still makes sense. Therefore, 'in the car' is likely to be a constituent; however we can't be certain yet. It is always important to do more than one constituency test to figure out if the word/words are constituents. It could pass one and fail the other three!

Next, let's do *replacement*. We take 'He sat down in the car' and replace 'in the car' with just one word. Useful words to try and use in a replacement test are *pronouns* (he, she, it, this, that etc).

'He sat down in the car.'

'He sat down there.'

The sentence makes sense once again! So 'in the car' has passed two constituency tests, but let's try another test first, just to make sure.

Time for the *standalone* test. We need to form a question using the rest of the sentence, and have the answer only be the word/words we are testing.

'Where did he sit down?'

'In the car.'

Success! It surely must be a constituent now. But we'll do the final test just in case. The final test is *movement*. Can we move the words we are testing to see if the sentence still makes sense?

'He sat down in the car.'

'It was in the car that he sat down.'

Once again the sentence makes sense. Now we have done these constituency tests, we know that 'in the car' is a constituent of the sentence 'He sat down in the car.' But be careful, *just because it is a constituent here does not mean it is a constituent in every other sentence*.

Relationships in Trees

So now we can identify constituents, let's go back to our tree. There are several important relationships in a syntax tree that we need to know about.

Domination – phrases can dominate words in a sentence tree. But how do we know which phrases dominate what? We said that a syntax tree has a **hierarchical** structure, which means that one label dominates all that is below it. Look at the picture below:

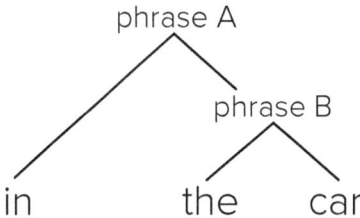

We can see here that phrase A dominates phrase B and 'in'. We know this because

SYNTAX 1

phrase A is above phrase B and it is above the word 'in'. When a phrase is directly above something, we call this **immediate domination**. Phrase A immediately dominates phrase B and 'in', but it does not immediately dominate 'the' or 'car'. But it is important to remember that even though it doesn't *immediately* dominate 'the' or 'car', it still dominates 'the' and 'car' because it is above them in the tree structure.

Naming Phrases

So, we looked before at verb phrases and noun phrases, but these aren't the only types of phrases you can have in a tree. We can also have adjective phrases, adverb phrases and prepositional phrases. We'll quickly talk about how these are different to the other phrases.

Adjective Phrases

Since phrases are named after the head, adjective phrases are simply phrases where the head of the phrase is an adjective. So for example the sentence 'The big red car drove away' contains the phrase 'The big red car'. This includes the adjectives 'big' and 'red'.

An adjective phrase can contain more than one adjective, so we can make 'big red' into a phrase.

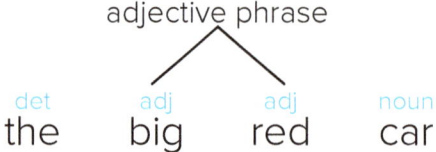

Next, we join this adjective phrase to the noun 'car' to make a noun phrase. But that's not all, since we have to add the determiner 'The' to complete the phrase. From there we can continue to build up the tree.

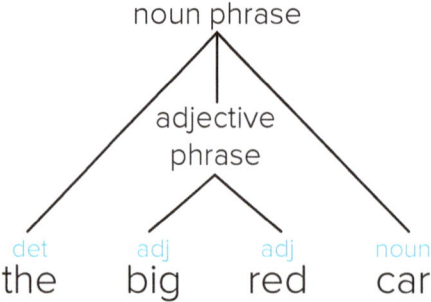

Adverb Phrases

These work a lot like adjective phrases. They are found near to verbs (because adverbs describe the verb), such as 'immediately' in the sentence 'he sat down immediately'. They are very easy to recognise, and often form adverb phrases containing just one word: the adverb itself. But be careful, adverbs can appear in a sentence and *not* be an adverb phrase! They are often used to modify an adjective, such as 'the immediately recognisable man'. Here, the adverb 'immediately' does not form an adverb phrase, but modifies the adjective in the adjective phrase 'immediately recognisable'.

Prepositional Phrases

Another type of phrase that is very common in sentence structures is the prepositional phrase. They may seem complicated at first but they will get easier to recognise with some practise. If we take the sentence 'The cat slept in the kitchen', we can break it down and analyse it to see where the prepositional phrase is.

Having labelled each word with its part of speech, we can see we have the preposition 'in' in this sentence. So let's start putting it together. Hopefully by now, you can see that 'the cat' is a noun phrase, and you can connect it. You should have seen that 'the kitchen' is also a noun phrase, and you can join it up as well.

Okay, so now let's join up 'in'. When we connect 'in' and the noun phrase 'the kitchen', we create a new phrase. This phrase is immediately dominating the noun phrase and the preposition 'in'. Therefore, we have made a preposition phrase. The noun phrase 'the kitchen' is modifying the location of where the cat slept, meaning it is modifying the word 'in'. So we know that 'in' is the head of this phrase, making it a preposition phrase.

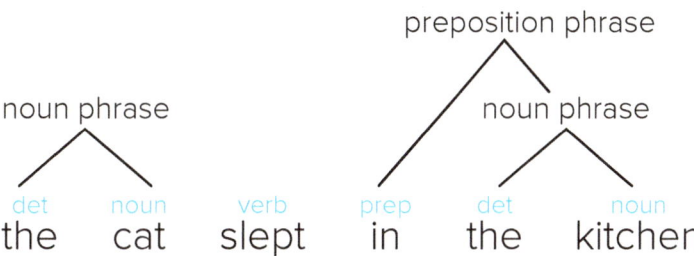

But we aren't quite finished yet! The preposition phrase 'in the kitchen' modifies the verb 'slept'. So we now join up the verb 'slept' and the preposition phrase 'in the kitchen' to make a new a phrase. Can you guess what phrase we make here?

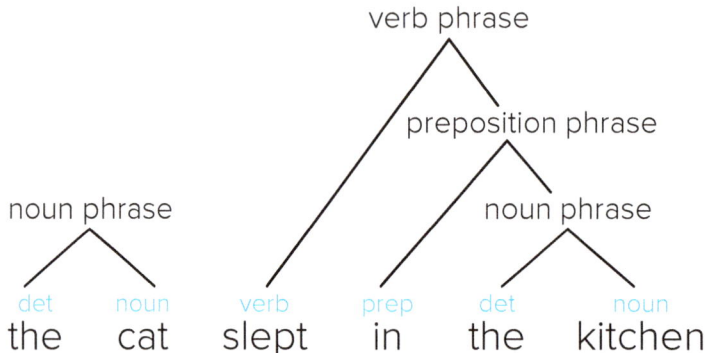

Yes, we make a verb phrase. This is because the verb is the head of the phrase and 'in the kitchen' modifies it. So now we have a noun phrase and a verb phrase left, and we can join them together to make a sentence.

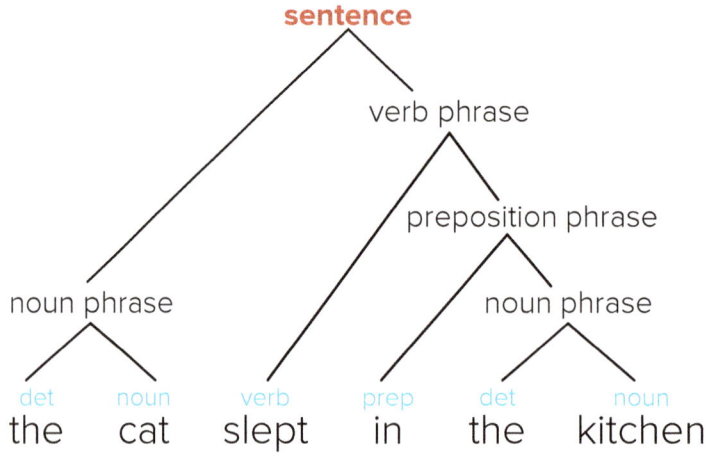

Usually when you want to join a word to a phrase, the word you are adding will be the head of the phrase, meaning that whatever part of speech it is, the phrase will be named after that part of speech. So if we join a noun to an adjective phrase, we will make a noun phrase. And if we join a verb to a noun phrase, we will make a verb phrase.

TUTORIAL 5.12

Co-ordinate Phrases

Co-ordinate phrases are rare phrases that do appear in English. You will have used them already, when you say things like 'fish and chips', 'Max and Ben', and pretty much any situation where you join two nouns together using the **conjunction** 'and'. So how do we deal with these?

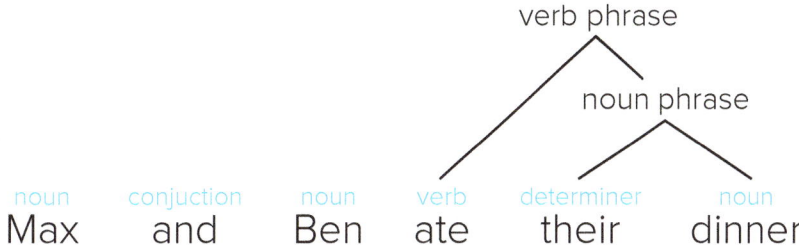

Here we have the sentence 'Max and Ben ate their dinner.' We have labelled the words, and we can construct the tree for the verb phrases, but we need to make a noun phrase for 'Max and Ben'. So how do we make the noun phrase? Well, 'Max' and 'Ben' are both proper nouns, meaning that they don't need a determiner. So here we just simply join 'Max', 'and', and 'Ben' together at the same time.

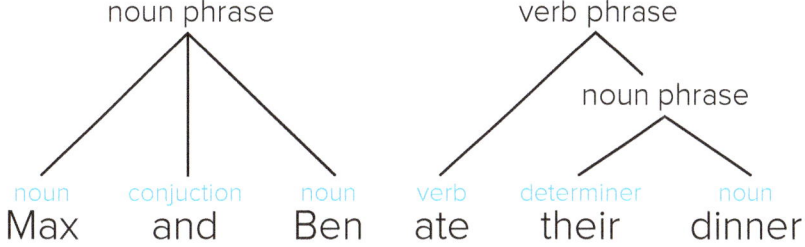

We can then label this as a noun phrase and join it to the verb phrase as a sentence.

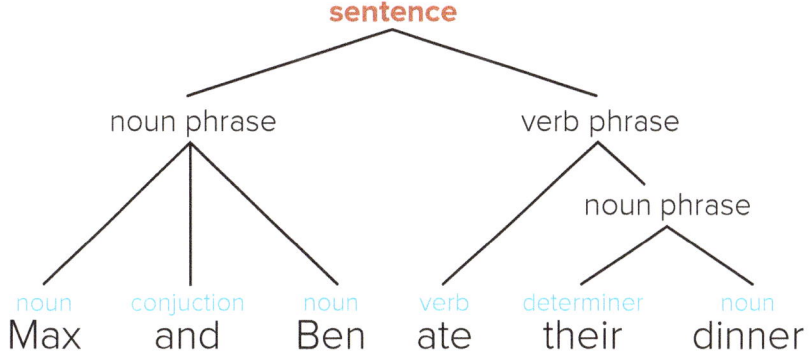

SYNTAX 1

But what if we don't have proper nouns? Let's take the sentence 'The boy and the girl ate their tea.' Again, we form the verb phrase, but what do we do to make the noun phrase? If you can work it out now, write it down and then check your answer with the tree below.

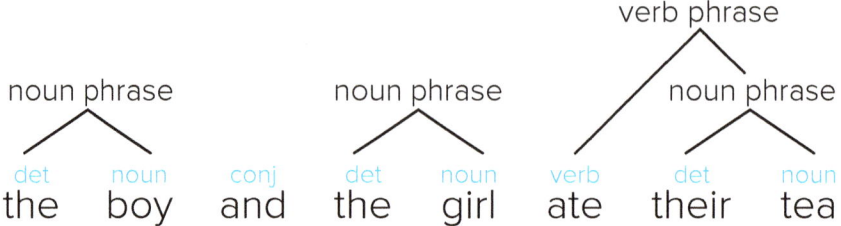

We created two separate noun phrases. We have the noun phrase 'the boy' and the noun phrase 'the girl', with 'and' sitting in the middle of them. Now, we can join them up like we did with the proper nouns, making a noun phrase that we can use to complete the sentence!

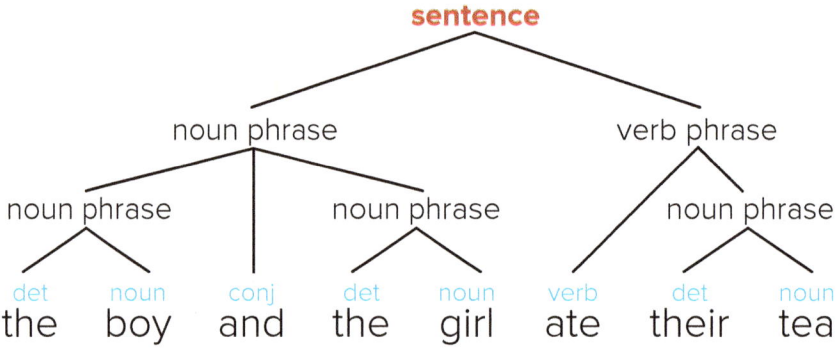

➡ ACTIVITIES

1. For the following phrases, name the head of the phrase:
   a. in the grass
   b. the cranky old woman
   c. ran as fast as he could
   d. jumped the fence
   e. that delicious meal

2. Using what you have learned, try to draw syntax tree diagrams for the following sentences.
   a. The dog ate the bone.
   b. My brother won the lottery.
   c. The boy kicked the ball.
   d. The dog saw a man in the park. (this one contains a Prepositional Phrase)
   e. The boy lives in the old house by the road. (this one is a bit more difficult, have a try at it, working systematically, but don't worry if you have to peek at the answer!)

3. Invent your own English sentence for the following syntax tree (answers will vary):

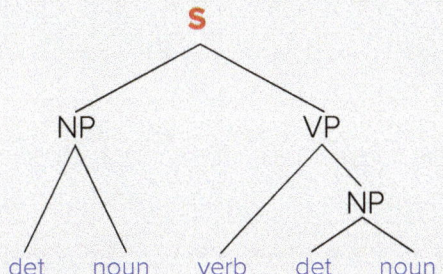

4. Determine if the following languages are VSO, SOV, OSV, etc.

Turkish:
Yusuf elmayı yedi
Yusuf the apple ate (Yusuf ate the apple.)

Arabic:
Qara'a l-mudarrisu l-kitāba.
Read the teacher the book (The teacher read the book.)

Hungarian:
Pista kenyeret szel
Pista bread slices (Pista slices bread.)

Biblical Hebrew:
Vayidaber YHWH el-Moshe
spoke YHWH to Moses (YHWH spoke to Moses)

Telegu:
Rāmuḍu baḍiki veḷtāḍu
Ramu to school goes (Ramu goes to school.)

Apurinã:
anana nota apa
pineapple I fetch (I fetch a pineapple.)

 **ANSWER**

1. The head of the phrase:
   a. in the <u>grass</u>,
   b. the cranky old <u>woman</u>,
   c. <u>ran</u> as fast as he could,
   d. <u>jumped</u> the fence,
   e. that delicious <u>meal</u>

2. Syntax tree diagrams:
   a. The dog ate the bone.

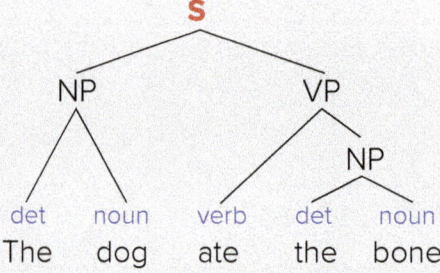

   b. My brother won the lottery.

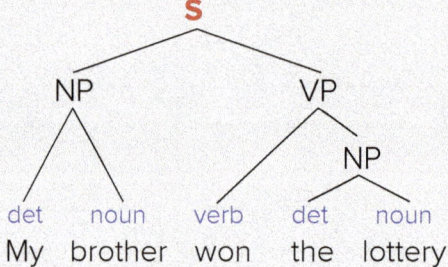

   c. The boy kicked the ball.

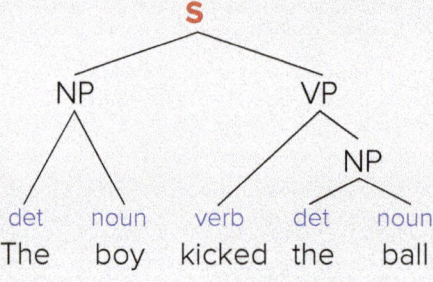

d. The dog saw a man in the park.

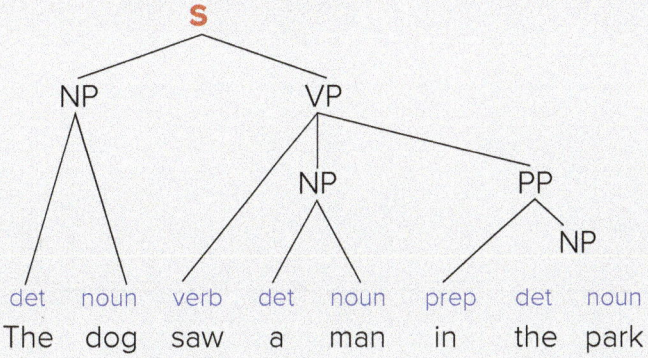

e. The boy lives in the old house by the road.

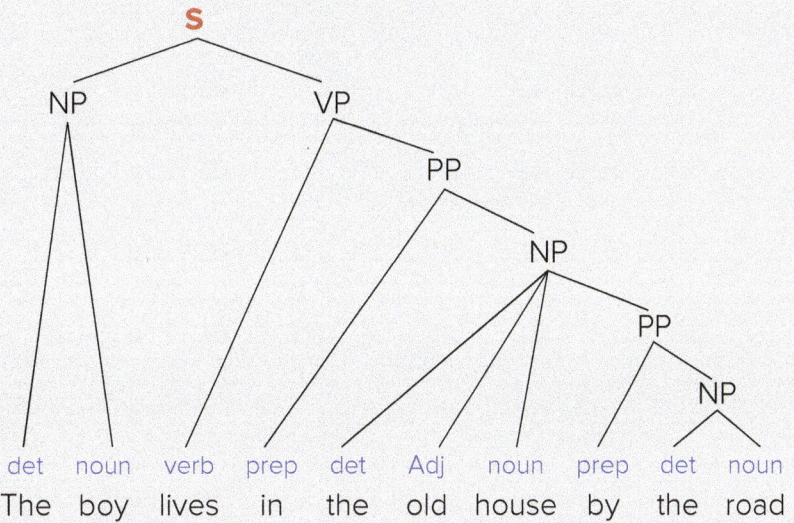

3. Answers will vary.

4. Sentence structure:

Turkish: SOV. Arabic: VSO. Hungarian: SOV.
Biblical Hebrew: VSO. Telegu: SOV. Apurinã: OSV.

5.13 Syntax 2

OBJECTIVES OF THIS TUTORIAL

This tutorial continues to discuss syntax - the unconscious principles people use to put words together into sentences.

Phrase structure in other languages

Every language has its own grammar, so phrase structure is different in different languages. The basic *principles* of how phrase structure works are universal and so are true for all languages. But the actual phrase structure in the syntax of different languages is what differs. Because the structure of sentences in different languages differs, the tree diagrams that represent those structures look very different:

English:

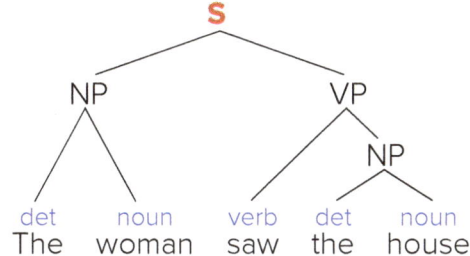

Fijian:

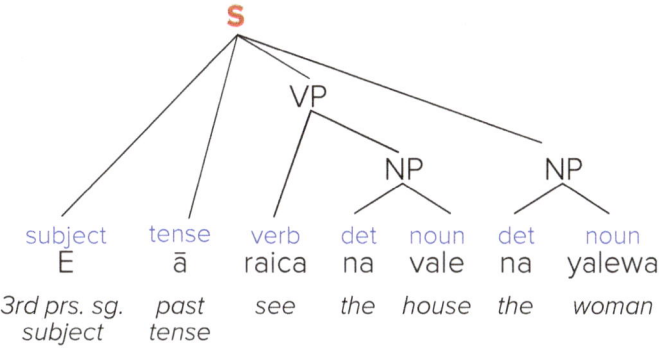

Fiji Hindi:

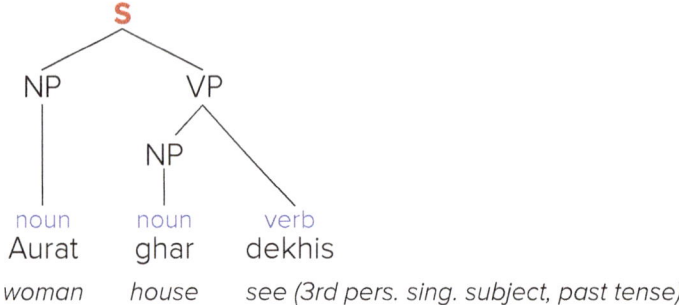

Most of the similarities between these trees relate to the way syntax works universally. The differences are to do with facts about the phrase structure of individual languages. One of the similarities between these different languages is that in each the verb and object are together in a Verb Phrase. Remember in the last tutorial we saw that over 90% of languages put the verb and object together, so they can form a Verb Phrase.

Remember also that language has a hierarchical structure. Constituents join together to build bigger constituents. A Verb Phrase consists of a verb and its object. A verb can join together with its object to build a Verb Phrase. But... only if the verb and object are next to each other. The verb and object Noun Phrase join together to form a larger constituent - the VP - before that then joins with the subject NP to make an even bigger unit - the sentence.

If the subject comes *between* the verb and the object there can't be a VP, like in the VSO language Maori. The Maori sentence below is - 'The man drank the water.'

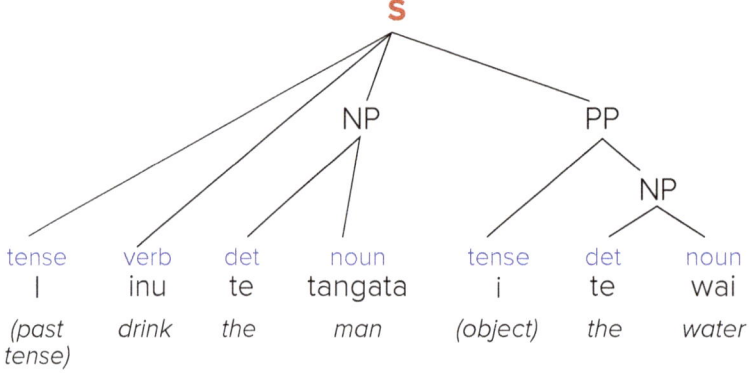

The fact that nearly 92% of languages are not like Maori, and instead put the verb and object together in a VP, shows us that languages prefer to combine constituents into larger constituents and have a hierarchical, nested structure.

Phrase structure rules

Phrases and sentences are constructed by speakers as they are speaking. Speakers generate phrases and sentences using the syntactic principles of the language they speak. These principles are unconscious rules stored in the minds of the speakers. We represent these principles as phrase structure rules. Together, the phrase structure rules of the language comprise the phrase structure grammar of the language.

As well as the phrasal rules, there is also a sentence rule – the rule about how to build a complete sentence out of these phrases. Traditionally linguists say that for English the sentence rule is basically this:

$S \rightarrow NP\ VP$

This means that a sentence consists of a NP (the subject) and a VP.

These rules are used to generate sentences. Believe it or not, every time we speak, our minds are going through a process - applying the phrase structure rules of our language and building phrases and sentences as they come out of our mouths. It is online generation of language. It takes a lot of mental processing power.

Heads and complements

You might remember in the last tutorial we said that in a phrase, we *must* have a word which is called the **head**. This is the core of the phrase, what the phrase can't exist without. It is the most important part of any phrase, because it is the part that gives the phrase its most important component of meaning.

So, in the phrase, *the really very ugly cat*, the head of the phrase is *cat* - the phrase is talking about a kind of cat, not a kind of ugliness. The head is where the phrase gets its category from - this is a NP because the head is a noun, *cat*.

Look at the phrase below: *the very ugly dogs inside the house*

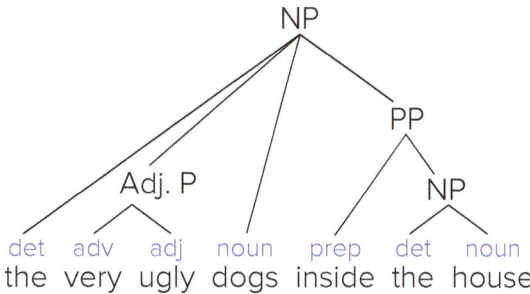

- *the very ugly dogs inside the house* is a Noun Phrase <u>because</u> its head is *dogs*, which is a noun;
- *very ugly* is an Adjective Phrase <u>because</u> its head is *ugly*, which is an adjective;
- *inside the house* is a Prepositional Phrase <u>because</u> its head is *inside*, which is a preposition.

Phrases have two main parts: a *head*, and a *complement* (this can also be called a *modifier*). The head is the part of the phrase that must be there (it's obligatory). You can have phrases without a complement, but you can't have a phrase without a head. A phrase is still a phrase even if it only has one word (its head) in it.

A phrase can also contain a complement, which is a phrase in itself, that tells us more about the head. Complements have to be there, but sometimes they are just implied - they complete the meaning of the head, and make the phrase grammatical. In the examples below, the example phrases are in brackets, and the head is in bold type.

	Head *does not* need a complement	Head *does* need a complement
NP	his [**appearance**]	[his **reliance** on email]
VP	The dog [**barked**].	The dog [**bit** the cat].
AP	Tom was [**happy**].	Tom was [**fond** of Mary].
PP	The monkey climbed [**in**].	The monkey climbed [**into** the house].

It is important to understand this concept of complements, because now we are going to talk about *argument structure*, which you will remember is the other important area of syntax along with phrase structure. Together, these two areas overlap and work together to provide the framework of principles that build meaning into sentences.

Argument Structure

Argument structure is all about how verbs relate to their complements and their subjects. Some constituents like Noun Phrases or Prepositional Phrases are complements – they are required by the verb. These are called *arguments* of the verb. The area of grammar that deals with this relationship is called argument structure.

Transitivity

Some verbs refer to events that involve only one participant. These verbs only require one argument. A verb like *sleep* only needs one argument, e.g., *Mary slept*. Other verbs, like *bite*, need two arguments, e.g., *The cat bit the dog.*

Then there are some verbs, like *give*, that need three arguments: *Mary gave the book to Tom.*

A sentence like 'Mary gave' is ungrammatical because it is incomplete – it's missing two of its arguments. Likewise, 'Mary gave the book', or 'Mary gave to Tom' or 'gave the book to Tom' are all ungrammatical because they are missing one of the three arguments they need.

This issue - how many arguments certain verbs need - is called *transitivity*.

Verbs like *sleep* that need only one argument are **intransitive**.

Verbs like *bite* that need two arguments are **transitive**.

Verbs like *give* that need three arguments are **ditransitive**.

Grammatical Relations

Each argument has a different *grammatical relation* – the job it has in relation to the verb in the sentence.

All verbs need a **subject**. So, if there is only one argument (as with an intransitive verb), that argument will be the subject. In an intransitive sentence like *Mary slept* the one argument is the subject (*Mary*). In a transitive sentence (where there are two arguments) like *The cat bit the dog,* one of the arguments (in this case *the cat*) is the subject, and the other (in this case *the dog*) is the **object**.

In a ditransitive sentence (where the verb needs three arguments) like *Mary gave Tom the book,* one of the arguments (in this case *Mary*) is the subject. The other two (*Tom* and *the book*) are both kinds of objects: Tom is an **indirect object**, and the book is a **direct object** (because it is having the verb *gave* done to it directly).

Other kinds of distransitive sentences have different grammatical relations. In the sentence, *Mary gave the book to Tom*, Tom now has the preposition *to* in front of him. Mary is still a subject, and the book is still a direct object. But Tom is now not an object, he's an **oblique**. Why? Because an object is a complement that is a Noun Phrase on its own (like *Tom* or *the book*). But an oblique is a complement that is a Prepositional Phrase (like *to Tom*).

So in summary, the *Grammatical Relations* are:
- subject
- object: direct object
  		indirect object
- oblique

Coding grammatical relations

The most important thing the grammar of a language has to be able to do is tell us which participant mentioned in a sentence is the subject, which is the object, etc. This is obviously a key to clearly communicating who is doing what to whom. This means a language has to have a way of expressing (or coding) the grammatical relation of each argument in a sentence.

In an intransitive sentence there is never any trouble working out who is the subject - there's only one argument, so that has to be the subject. We always know who the subject is in *Mary slept*, because there's only Mary.

SYNTAX 2

But, in a transitive sentence how do we know which of the arguments is the subject and which is the object? In *The cat bit the dog,* how do we know that *the cat* is the subject, and not *the dog*? There are three ways languages can code grammatical relations so we know which is the subject and which is the object:

- word order
- case marking
- agreement

We will look at each of these three and explain how languages use them.

Word order

In English the main way grammatical relations are coded is by word order. The subject comes before the verb, and the object comes after it. That's why we say that English has the basic sentence structure SVO:

The cat bit the dog.
    S   V   O

Other languages also use word order to show grammatical relations, but the order is different to English. For example, in Arabic, the sentence structure is VSO:

Qara'a   al-mudarrisu   al-kitaba
read   det-teacher   det-book
V   S   O

'The teacher read the book.'

Case

Case involves attaching an affix or an adposition (a preposition or a postposition) to the noun to tell us its grammatical relation. In Latin it doesn't matter what order the nouns are in – instead the nouns have a suffix that tells us their grammatical relation:

Domin-us vidit lup-um.	Domin-um vidit lup-us.
master-SUBJ see wolf-OBJ	master-OBJ see wolf-SUBJ
'The master sees the wolf.'	'The wolf sees the master.'

The noun that is the subject has the case marker *-us*, the noun that is the object has the case marker *-um*. All of the following sentences mean '*The master sees the wolf*' in Latin, it doesn't matter that the word order is switched, as long as the case markers are correct the meaning is clear.

>Lup-um domin-us vidit.
>wolf-OBJ master-SUBJ see
>'The master sees the wolf.'

>Domin-us lup-um vidit.
>master-SUBJ wolf-OBJ see
>'The master sees the wolf.'

>Vidit domin-us lup-um.
>see master-SUBJ wolf-OBJ
>'The master sees the wolf.'

English has no case marking on nouns. For example, *The cat bit the dog* and *The dog bit the cat*. In both sentences *the cat* is just *the cat*, whether it's the subject or the object, it doesn't change form at all. The same is true with *the dog*. But, English does have case marking on pronouns:

>*I saw her.*
>*She saw me.*

We only say *I* or *she* if the person is the subject.
We only say *me* or *her* if the person is the object.

Agreement

Agreement involves attaching something to the verb to tell us which argument is the subject and which one is the object. In English we don't have much verb agreement, only the suffix –s:

>*I see her.*
>*She sees me.*

The suffix -s tells us that the subject is third person singular (*he, she* or *it*). The suffix agrees with the subject.

In some other languages agreement is much more important than in English and does all the work. In a language like that, word order might not matter, like in Latin, where the case markers did all the work of making the subject and objects clear. Look carefully at the example sentences below from Yimas (Sepik, Papua New Guinea). All of these sentences mean "*The men saw the woman*":

pay-um narmaŋ na-mpu-**tay**
man-PL woman   femSG.OBJ-mascPL.SBJ-see

narmaŋ **pay-um** na-mpu-**tay**
woman   man-PL   femSG.OBJ-mascPL.SBJ-see

pay-um na-mpu-**tay**   **narmaŋ**
man-PL   femSG.OBJ-mascPL.SBJ-see   woman

narmaŋ na-mpu-**tay**   **pay-um**
woman   femSG.OBJ-mascPL.SBJ-see   man-PL

na-mpu-**tay**   **narmaŋ** **pay-um**
femSG.OBJ-mascPL.SBJ-see   woman   man-PL

na-mpu-**tay**   **pay-um** **narmaŋ**
femSG.OBJ-mascPL.SBJ-see   man-PL   woman

In Yimas all nouns belong to a noun class. In the example sentences the first prefix attached to the verb agrees with the noun class and the number (singular or plural) of the argument. The order of the actual nouns in relation to the verbs doesn't matter.

Semantic roles

All arguments have a grammatical relation. But all arguments also have a *semantic role* - or a role in the *meaning*. The most important semantic roles are: *actor* and *undergoer*.

An actor 'does' the action, and is directly responsible for the event. An undergoer has the action happen to them.

Actors

There are three kinds of actors:
- agent
- force
- cause

The most important kind of actor is **agent**. An agent does something on purpose. They are usually human, but can sometimes be an animal:

The boy killed the cobra.

The cat caught the bird.

Agents often do something that affects a second argument (e.g., *the cobra, the bird*). They can also perform an act that does not involve a second argument: e.g. *The boy hurried.*
A **force** performs the action, but not intentionally:

Malaria killed the boy.

The storm destroyed the crops.

A **cause** doesn't perform an action, it causes the action to happen:

The delay disrupted the schedule.

The rain kept the boys indoors.

Undergoers

Here are some examples of sentences with undergoers marked - the undergoer is the person or thing having the action done to it. Undergoers can also be undergoing a change of state or location, or be described as being in a particular state or location.

The boy killed the cobra.

Tom cooked the chicken.

The cobra is dead.

The chicken is cooked.

The pen is on the desk.

The book is on the ground.

Tom put the pen on the desk.

The book fell onto the ground.

Some other important semantic roles

There are quite a few other *semantic roles*, and not all linguists agree on them all. Your goal is only to understand that these kinds of relationships between words and meaning exist, and that they differ in the way they work in different languages.

We will look at some of the most important and generally accepted ones, giving a short explanation and a few examples.

Benefactive and recipient (Dative)

A *benefactive* is someone or something who benefits from the event. In English benefactives are marked with the preposition *for* (*for* also has other jobs).

>Tom cooked a meal *for Mary*.
>
>The boys bought a book *for their sister*.

A *recipient* is someone or something who receives something as a result of the event. In English recipients are marked with the preposition *to* (it too also has other jobs).

>Nick passed a note *to Melissa*.
>
>The salesman gave a brochure *to the customer*.

Many languages treat benefactives and recipients in the same way. This is called *dative*.

Experiencer

An *experiencer* experiences or senses a mental, emotional, physical or sensory state. Experiencers are always animate (alive), usually human:

>*Alfredo* likes chips.
>
>*The old man* feels sick.
>
>*We* thought they had left.

English has some pairs of sensory verbs, one with an agent, one with an experiencer:

AGENT	EXPERIENCER
Mary *watched* the fight.	Mary *saw* the fight.
Tom *listened* to the announcement.	Tom *heard* the announcement.
The visitor *smelled* the rotten fish.	The visitor *smelled* the rotten fish.

(The last example, *smelled*, fits both categories as an agent and an experiencer)

Stimulus

A *stimulus* is the counterpart to an experiencer – it is the cause of the experience.

>Mary saw *the fight*.
>
>Tom heard *the announcement*.
>
>The visitor smelled *the rotten fish*.

Instrument

An instrument is used by an actor to perform the action:

The hammer broke the window.
The key opened the door.
The bullet killed Tom.

In English instruments can be paraphrased with a Prepositional Phrase using 'with'.

Locationals

There are several different locationals. The four most important types are:

- **locative** (the location where an event happens) *Louisa waited in the pub*.
- **goal** (the end point of an event) *Nick drove to the shop*.
- **source** (the starting point of an event) *The robbers left the bank*.
- **temporal** (location in time when an event happens) *I arrived last week*.

In English locationals can be expressed by Noun Phrases, Prepositional Phrases, or adverbs. English uses different prepositions to express different kinds of locationals.

Semantic Roles and Grammatical Relations

Semantic Roles are not the same thing as grammatical relations. Grammatical relations can't be defined on the basis of meaning.

Actors are usually subjects and undergoers are usually objects, but they don't *have* to be.

Subjects can have a range of semantic roles (roles in the meaning of a sentence):

The boy killed the cobra. (agent)
The boy enjoyed the film. (experiencer)
The storm destroyed the house. (force)
Rain stopped the game. (cause)
The cobra was killed by the boy. (undergoer)
The cobra is dead. (undergoer)
The coconut fell to the ground. (undergoer)
The key unlocked the door. (instrument)
Bats inhabit these caves. (undergoer)
Louisa received a parcel. (recipient)

Objects can have a range of semantic roles too:
> *The boy killed <u>the cobra</u>.* (undergoer)
> *The boy enjoyed <u>the film</u>.* (cause)
> *The boy dropped <u>the coconut</u>.* (undergoer)
> *The delay upset <u>Louisa</u>.* (experiencer)
> *The train approached <u>the station</u>.* (goal)
> *The bus left <u>the university</u>.* (source)

Passive and active sentences

Languages have quite a few ways of changing the argument structure of a sentence. One important way is by using a *passive construction*.

In sentences with an ordinary transitive verb like *kill* or *bite* the subject is an actor. The object also has a semantic role: it is an undergoer.

For example, in a sentence like *John killed the mosquito*:
- John has the semantic role of agent, and the grammatical relation of subject;
- The mosquito has the semantic role of undergoer, and the grammatical relation of object.

But, this changes if we switch the sentence around. Let's have a look:

The mosquito was killed by John.
- The mosquito still has the semantic role of undergoer, but now it has the grammatical relation of subject.
- John still has the semantic role of actor, but now he isn't even an object – because he has a preposition (*by*), he is now an oblique.

We can even leave the oblique (*John*) out completely: *The mosquito was killed.*

The issue here is what we call **voice**.

The sentence *John killed the mosquito* is in *active voice*.

The sentence *The mosquito was killed (by John)* is in *passive voice*.

Active sentences are more basic than passive sentences because:
- the actor is the subject (they are functionally more basic); and
- they are grammatically less complicated.

Passive sentences are grammatically more complicated:
- they have an auxiliary verb *be* (actually also often *got*); and
- the actor is in a prepositional phrase with *by*, instead of just being a noun phrase.

So, if a passive sentence has basically the same meaning as an active sentence, why do languages have a passive structure at all? Basically, passives exist so we can manipulate the way information is presented. Passives are used for two reasons:

1. To emphasise the undergoer: e.g., *Tom was run over by a car* - we say it that way because we are interested in Tom and not in the car. We make Tom the subject and the car is demoted to an oblique. We may even get rid of the car altogether and just say, *Tom was run over*.
2. To push the actor into the background. We might want to do this because we don't know who the actor is: *My car was stolen* (I don't know who stole it); or maybe we don't care who the actor is: *The parcel was delivered* (I don't care who delivered it); or maybe we don't want to say who the actor is: *Your application was rejected* (by me, but I don't want to tell you that).

ACTIVITIES

1. Change each of the passive voice sentences below to active voice:
   a. A piece of wood had been swallowed by the dog.
   b. Two separate customers were given rides on the new motorbikes by the designer.
   c. Our child is frightened by loud fireworks.
   d. The old door was painted bright red by the woman's daughter.
   e. Finances for the project were not included in the budget by the committee.
   f. The vibrant colours of the sculpture are immediately noticed by art gallery visitors.

2. Fill in the blanks in the following notes to review what you have learned in the last two Tutorials.

Syntax: Study Notes
1. The unconscious principles which people use to put words together into sentences are called the _____ of a language.
2. The two main areas of syntax which overlap and connect are _____ _____ and _____ _____ .
3. The _____ _____ of a language is the set of principles about how words are put together to make phrases, and how words and phrases are put together to build sentences.

SYNTAX 2

4. _____ _____ is about the way the participants are expressed in the grammar of a sentence.
5. The main parts of a sentence are the _____ (S), _____ (O) and _____ (V).
6. There are _____ possible orders for these parts to be arranged in a sentence.
7. The combinations _____ and _____ occur in 88.2% of the world's languages.
8. Languages overwhelmingly like to have the _____ first.
9. 91.6% of languages have the _____ and _____ occurring together.
10. When the verb and object occur together there can be a _____ .
11. _____ are the most basic building blocks that are used to build sentences.
12. They are the component parts, or _____ of a sentence.
13. Words group together into larger units called _____ .
14. There are several different types of phrase that can be used in a sentence, but the two phrases which *must* be used in a sentence for it to make sense are a _____ _____ and a _____ _____ .
15. In a phrase, we *must* have a word which is called the _____ . This is the core of the phrase, what the phrase can't exist without.
16. Words join together to form larger _____ .
17. There are various ways to test whether or not a series of words form a single constituent:
    a) _____ – Create the same sentence but take away the word/words we are testing.
    b) _____ – Can we replace the word/words with just a single word?
    c) _____ – Can we form a question using the sentence, and the answer be the word/words being tested?
    d) _____ – Can we move the position of the word/words in the sentence and have the sentence still make sense without changing the meaning?
18. Speakers generate _____ and _____ using the syntactic principles of the language they speak.
19. These unconscious principles are called _____ _____ _____ .

20. The most basic phrase structure rules generate the basic phrase structure of head, followed by _____ .
21. Some constituents such as Noun Phrases or Prepositional Phrases are complements – they are required by the _____ .
22. These are called _____ of the verb.
23. Some verbs refer to events that involve only one participant. These verbs only require one _____ (e.g. *Mary went to* sleep)
24. Other verbs require _____ arguments (e.g. *The cat* bit *the dog*)
25. Some verbs require _____ arguments (e.g. *Mary* gave *the book to Tom*)
26. This issue is called _____ .
27. Verbs like *sleep* that need only one argument are _____ .
28. Verbs like *bite* that need two arguments are _____ .
29. Verbs like *give* that need three arguments are _____ .
30. There are three ways languages can code grammatical relations so we know which is the subject and which is the object: _____ _____ , _____ _____ , _____ .
31. The most important semantic roles are _____ and _____ .
32. An _____ 'does' the action, and is directly responsible for the event.
33. An _____ has the action happen to them.
34. *The mosquito was killed by John*, is a sentence using the _____ voice.

SYNTAX 2

✓ ANSWERS

1. Passive voice sentences changed to active voice:
   a. The dog had swallowed a piece of wood.
   b. The designer gave two separate customers rides on the new motorbikes.
   c. Loud fireworks frighten our child.
   d. The woman's daughter painted the old door bright red.
   e. The committee did not include finances for the project in the budget.
   f. Art gallery visitors immediately noticed the vibrant colours of the sculpture.

2. Syntax: study notes answers
   1. syntax
   2. phrase structure, argument structure
   3. phrase structure
   4. Argument structure
   5. subject (S), object (O) and verb (V)
   6. six
   7. SOV, SVO
   8. subject
   9. verb, object
   10. Verb Phrase
   11. Words
   12. constituents
   13. phrases
   14. noun phrase, verb phrase
   15. head
   16. constituents
   17. a) Omission
       b) Replacement
       c) Standalone
       d) Movement
   18. phrases, sentences

19. phrase structure rules
20. complement
21. verb
22. arguments
23. argument
24. two
25. three
26. transitivity
27. intransitive
28. transitive
29. ditransitive
30. word order, case marking, agreement
31. actor, undergoer
32. actor
33. undergoer
34. passive

5.14 Language and Meaning

OBJECTIVES OF THIS TUTORIAL

This tutorial discusses how language contains and communicates meaning, and what meaning actually is. It uses an illustration from a Native American culture to explore some key issues in language, meaning and identity.

Introduction

We could say that communication is:

A two-way process of reaching mutual understanding, in which participants not only exchange news, information, ideas and feelings but also create and share meaning.

But in practical terms, how do we actually create meaning? And what are the factors involved in sharing what we mean with another person, and for us to understand what they mean?

Since we are going to focus on meaning in the next group of tutorials, we should probably try to come up with a simple definition first. But, apparently a simple definition is difficult to come up with - *"Philosophers have debated the question [i.e. of what meaning is], with particular reference to language, for well over 2000 years. No one has yet produced a satisfactory answer to it."* (Lyons, 1981)

But even though philosophers haven't pinned it down yet (maybe if we give them another 2000 years...), we still have a pretty good idea of what meaning is. We might have trouble *defining* it, but we probably all have some sense of what it *is* - we are able to understand sentences such as:

What is the *meaning* of malophile? or

What does malophile *mean*? [*in case you are wondering ... 'one who loves apples'*]

and we can ask and understand similar questions about other languages:

What is the meaning (in English) of (the Ata word) *lavuxi*? [*banana*] or

What does *casa* (the Spanish word) mean in English? [*house*]

LANGUAGE AND MEANING

If we know the word or the language involved, we can answer these kinds of questions, which shows that we *do* know at some level what *meaning* is, even if we can't put it into words.

Semantics and Pragmatics

We said before that communication involves creating and sharing meaning. When we listen to someone speaking we are trying to understand what they *mean* by what they are saying. This is actually a very complicated process, and it doesn't just involve the words being spoken, or the way those words are put together into sentences, but it also involves other things like the relationship we have with the person speaking, their cultural background and the social context we are in. All of these considerations in the area of meaning in language are together referred to as *semantics* and *pragmatics*.

"It has been generally assumed that we have to understand two types of meaning to understand what the speaker means by uttering a sentence. . . . A sentence expresses a more or less complete propositional content, which is semantic meaning, and extra pragmatic meaning comes from a particular context in which the sentence is uttered." (Etsuko Oishi, 2003)

Semantics is the structured system of meaning within individual languages. It is the way the grammar and lexicon (the vocabulary or units of meaning) of a language construct meaning in words, and sentences, and the way parts of sentences relate to each other in terms of meaning. Native speakers have an unconscious knowledge of the operation of semantics - of meaning in their language. Semantics is the part of grammar that builds meaning, and controls the relationship between meanings of words and phrases.

Pragmatics is concerned with the use of language in real interaction in real social contexts and the ways in which people produce and comprehend meanings through language. Some examples might be asking someone to "put the kettle on", when you really want them to make you a cup of coffee, or saying that "it's a cold day today", when you want them to close the window. Pragmatics looks at the practical aspects of human action and thought, and the use of linguistic signs (words and sentences), in actual situations.

Why is this important?

We will be looking at semantics and pragmatics in more detail in the next tutorials and discover the 'nuts and bolts' of how they work. But first we want to start with a bigger picture of the importance of this area to cross-cultural communicators. Probably you can already see why it is important for those whose goal is to communicate spiritual truth into another language and cultural situation, to have a good understanding of how meaning is created and shared in that context.

? DISCUSSION POINTS

1. Pick a language you do not speak, but are able to do some research about online. Why do people who speak this language consider their language important: e.g. what specific things are they not able to express any other way, which areas they can only speak about in the language, and what the language means to them in terms of their identity.

2. How do you think these issues of identity and language could affect the message and messengers who might come from outside and try to present Truth in that setting?

5.15 Semantics 1

OBJECTIVES OF THIS TUTORIAL

This tutorial introduces semantics - the structured system of meaning within individual languages. We will begin by looking at lexical semantics, or the meaning that is contained in words and expressions.

Introduction

In the last tutorial we looked at the 'big picture' of language and meaning, and all the factors that help us to create and share meaning when we communicate with someone else. Now we are going to focus on *semantics*, which is the structured system of meaning within individual languages. It is the way the grammar and lexicon of a language construct meaning in words, and sentences, and the way parts of sentences relate to each other in terms of meaning.

A native speaker of a language has an unconscious knowledge of the operation of meaning in their language. They know, without thinking about it, how to use grammar to build meaning, and they unconsciously control the relationship between meanings of words and phrases. But, because it is a structured system that follows particular rules and patterns, we can look at the semantics of a language and see how that system works.

Semantics is the part of grammar that tells us there is a special relationship between *short* and *tall* in a way that there isn't between *short* and *forgetful*. It tells us that it is impossible to *meet a man who wasn't there* because the meaning of the word *meet* means the person who gets *met* must be present.

Semantics tells us that a *giant turtle larger than a house* is OK (unusual, but OK in a sci-fi movie), but it rules out a *giant hill larger than a mountain* (even though normal hills are already much larger than turtles), because the word *hill* includes in its meaning that it's smaller than a mountain, while the word *turtle* does not include anything in its meaning about its relationship in size to houses.

The Lexicon

For a native speaker, each word or expression in their language has a lot of information attached to it - for instance they know how to pronounce it, they know how it operates in the syntax, they know the variety of possible meanings it has and they know how it interacts with other words or expressions to change its meaning in certain circumstances. All of this information about words and expressions is stored in the *mental lexicon* of the speaker of the language. The lexicon is a store of all the relevant information about words and expressions that a person needs to know to be able to use them correctly to convey meaning.

This semantic information about each word or expression (also called a *lexeme*) is contained in the mental lexicon of each language.

Denotation versus connotation

When we talk about 'meaning' we are usually talking about something called *denotation*. Denotation is the literal meaning of a word or sentence.

When we say the word *dog* it denotes an entity in the world that we could refer to as 'a canine animal'. Denotation is the linguistic form's descriptive, or literal meaning.

As well as having a literal meaning, words or expressions can also have other meanings, other *connotations*. Connotation refers to the emotional associations, social overtones or cultural implications that are part of the meaning of a word or expression, over and above its purely descriptive content.

Words convey more than their exact, literal meanings - they *connote* or suggest additional meanings and values as well. Sometimes, because of usage over time, words that *denote* approximately the same thing they always did, may acquire additional meanings, or *connotations*, that are either positive or negative. Consider the changes undergone in the connotations of these words in the 20th century: liberal, diversity, right wing, follower, gay, minority, feminist, left wing, abuse, conservative, motherhood, extremist, rights, partner, harassment, family, propaganda, peacekeeper, and comrade.

Social meaning

Sometimes words or expressions also connote *social meaning*. The social meaning of a linguistic form is what that form tells the hearer about the social characteristics of the speaker - their class, level of education, gender, regional background, ethnicity and so on. For example, in Australia if I said to some friends, "Are yous gunna come with us, or what?" I would probably be considered 'rough' and assumptions might be made about my class or education. It could make some people uncomfortable, but others may feel more comfortable with me.

There are a lot of social meaning connotations that can be made when we hear someone's speech - things like their age, gender, regional background, ethnicity or subculture.

Affective meaning

The affective meaning of a linguistic form tells the hearer about the *attitudes* of the speaker. It can tell you how they feel about what they are talking about, just by the words they choose. For example, choosing one or the other of these words shows a different attitude:

- *brave* vs. *reckless*
- *strong willed* vs. *pig-headed*
- *fat* vs. *well-built*
- *police officer* vs. *constable* vs. *cop* vs. *pig*
- *skinny* vs. *slender*

Factors such as stress and intonation can also show *affective meaning*. Sarcasm can be expressed just by using a different intonation:

Oh yeah, that was a really clever thing to do! (With two different intonation patterns.)

In any language, separating grammatical denotation from connotation is important because while you might understand a word's denotation, knowing a word's connotations and what they are intended for, is much more difficult to know. Connotations are often emotional in nature, and if they are intended, it could be for any number of purposes - to sway opinion one way or another, to communicate a personal identity, or to share a deep feeling.

If there are misunderstandings about how a person is using a particular word, a primary source of that misunderstanding might lie in the word's connotations: people might be seeing something not intended, or the speaker may be intending something people don't see. In cross-cultural communication, it's obviously extremely important not merely to look at what your words and other's words *denote*, but also what they *connote*.

Semantic relations

Polysemy and homonymy

This sounds complicated, but it actually isn't. Homonymy or polysemy just refer to the fact that one group of sounds can have more than one meaning.

Homonyms are unrelated lexemes that just happen to have the same form:

- *bank* (of a river) vs. *bank* (financial institution)
- *keep* (to retain) vs. *keep* (of a castle)
- *bow* (of a boat) vs. *bow* (bend forward) etc.

Homophones are homonyms that are pronounced the same, regardless of how they are written:
- *bow* (front of a boat) vs. *bough* (branch of a tree)
- *I* (me) vs. *eye* (that sees)
- *to* (towards) vs. *too* (also)

Homographs are homonyms that are written the same way, regardless of whether they are pronounced the same:
- *wind* (that blows) vs. *wind* (twist)
- *bow* (of a boat) vs. *bow* (for arrows)

Many homonyms are both a homophone and a homograph (*bank* and *bank* are both). *Wring* and *ring* are homophones but not homographs. *Bow* (of a boat) and *bow* (for arrows) are homographs but not homophones.

Polysemy involves a word that has more than one meaning, but they are different senses of the same word. A single lexeme may have several 'meanings', for example, *bank* can mean:
- a financial institution,
- a building,
- the dealer and distributor of money in gambling games,
- to deposit money in a financial institution,
- to depend on; etc.

Other examples are:
- *mouth*: *mouth* of a river, *mouth* of a person.
- *lose: lose* a football match, *lose* your keys

The lexical information for words such as *bank* contains information that this lexeme has several senses – various closely related and overlapping meanings that it can have. An example of polysemy in Bengali is the word māthāy

1. chabiṭā ṭebiler **māthāy** rākho
   "Keep the picture on the table"
2. tomār kathāṭā āmār **māthāy** āche
   "Your word is in my mind"
3. tin diner **māthāy** tini phire elen
   "He returned by the beginning of the 3rd day"

In the examples given above, the Bengali word māthāy, is used in three different senses: in (1), it means 'top of a table', in (2), it implies 'mind of a person', and in (3), it indicates 'beginning of a day'. In Bengali, these senses are concepts that are related in meaning, and māthāy is considered to be one lexeme that can be used to express many different senses (more than are illustrated in our examples here).

Antonymy and synonymy

Words or utterances that have the same meaning are **synonyms**. Some examples of synonyms are: *quick* and *fast*; *big* and *large*; *movie* and *film*; *rent* and *hire*. There are a lot of different reasons why certain synonyms are used and when they are used, here are some examples:

Synonyms may belong to different *registers* (they would be used by different people in different situations):

- *hubby* vs. *husband* vs. *spouse*
- *pet* vs. *companion animal*
- *grabbed* vs. *nicked* vs. *apprehended*
- *mouth* vs. *oral cavity*
- *tell* vs. *inform*,
- *police officer* vs. *cop*

Synonyms may have different *connotative* meaning (so people would choose the one that best expressed their meaning):

- *police officer* vs. *pig*
- *talked* vs. *droned on* vs. *enthralled*
- *brave* vs. *reckless*
- *swamp* vs. *wetlands*

Synonyms may be used in different *linguistic* situations:

- *rented/hired*: "They *rented/hired* a car", but "They *rented* a house", and "They *hired* a new receptionist".
- *pair/couple*: "a *pair/couple* of dogs", but "a *pair* of trousers", and "a *couple* of dollars".

Synonyms may have different *semantic* range:
- *boss* and *employer*: If you work in a small business your *boss* may also be your *employer*. In a large organization your *boss* may be a fellow employee who is your manager, while your *employer* is the organization, which you would not refer to as your *boss*.

Synonyms may have different *dialectal* or *sociolectal* distribution (they may be used in different regions or by different groups in society):
- *footpath* vs. *sidewalk* vs. *pavement*
- *couch* vs. *sofa* vs. *settee* vs. *lounge*
- *chap* vs. *fellow* vs. *bloke* vs. *dude*
- *gun* vs. *piece* vs. *weapon* vs. *sidearm*

Words or utterances that have the *opposite* meaning are **antonyms**. Some examples of antonyms are: *quick* vs. *slow*; *big* vs. *small*, *hot* vs. *cold*.

Some antonyms are *complementary*, which means they are absolute and mutually exclusive and mean the exact opposite of one another.
- *alive* vs. *dead*
- *married* vs. *unmarried*
- *hit* vs. *miss*

One rules out the other - if something is *alive*, that means that it is *not dead*. So, part of the meaning of *dead* is '*not alive*'. We could say that a pair of complementary antonyms exhausts the full range of possibilities - something is either one or the other.

But, some antonyms are *gradable* antonyms. These are antonyms but they have shades or degrees of meaning between them:
- *big* vs. *small* (A mouse might be big in relation to a flea, but small in relation to a cow)
- *new* vs. *old*
- *hot* vs. *cold* (A cup of coffee is hot compared to ice but cold compared to magma. A cup of coffee can be a bit hot or not very hot. One cup of coffee can be hot, another hotter, and yet another the hottest)

Some words have opposite meanings that are *reverses*:
- *push* vs. *pull*
- *increase* vs. *decrease*

Some pairs of words have *converse* meanings. These kinds of words are '*converses*' or '*relational opposites*':
- *mother* vs. *daughter* (If Linda is Dania's *mother*, then Dania is Linda's *daughter*)
- *buy* vs. *sell* (If Paul *sells* the car to Bob, then Bob *buys* the car from Paul)

Some individual words have their own converse meanings too:
- *rent* (If Jim *rents* a house to Simon, Simon *rents* the house from Jim).

Metaphor

We saw that with *polysemy*, one word (one lexeme stored in our minds) can have several closely connected meanings. But there is another possibility if a word seems to have two meanings: it could be that one of the meanings is the literal (or 'real') meaning, and the other is using the word to refer to something else, knowing that it is not really what we are saying. This second kind of use is a *metaphor*. Let's look at some examples.

A **wave** of emotion **swept over** him.

We all know what a *wave* is ('a moving wall of water'), and what *swept* means, and what *over* means. But when we say that sentence, we don't mean that a wall of something moved across the top of the person. A metaphor is simply using a word that means one thing to refer to something else. We use metaphors because we want to suggest that in some way it is like the thing it normally refers to. A wall of water in the ocean is something bigger than us that we can't control, and emotion can be that way as well, so we use the metaphor of a sweeping wave to express that idea of helplessness.

*An idea **hit** him.*

We don't mean the idea punched him. We mean that when he thought of the idea, he thought of it suddenly, and it had a big impact on him – that thinking of it was in some ways a bit like being punched – it had suddenness and impact.

Some metaphors are so commonly used that we don't even notice them. For example we often say, "*I see what you mean.*" Using *see* to mean '*understand*' is so common in English that we don't even notice it as a metaphor - there are many of these in English.

Metaphors don't need to just involve individual words. They can be organized into whole lexical domains (or areas of meaning), where one area is used to talk about another. One example of this is talking about *time* as if it was *money*:

You're wasting my time.
Is that worth your while?
This gadget will save you hours.
He's living on borrowed time.
How do you spend your time?
You don't use your time profitably.
You need to budget your time.

Another example is talking about *ideas or plans* as if they involved *cooking*:

He's full of half-baked ideas.
We've got that one on the boil.
What scheme are you cooking up?
They put that plan on the backburner.

Metaphors are cultural

Metaphors reflect cultural perspectives, and different cultures use different *metaphorical domains*. For example, English treats the *heart* as the place in the body where emotion is:

He has a lighthearted attitude to life.
The news left him with a heavy heart.
They offered their heartfelt thanks.
He's got a good heart.
He's a brave hearted fellow.
They were heartbroken.

In many other languages emotion is located in the *stomach* (sometimes in the *liver*). For example in Ata (Papua New Guinea):

- opoleli tu'umaxu (*my stomach is heavy* - 'I am sad')
- oponu ukunikuni (*his stomach is trembling* - 'he is afraid')
- opoleli laixe (*my stomach is good* - 'I am OK, at peace')
- muto'omolu oponu (*it speared his stomach* - 'it convicted him')

Metaphors of space and time

An important source of metaphor involves *spatial* terms, and terms for physical space are used as metaphors for many things.

One important example is *space* as a metaphor for *time*. In some languages the future is treated as in front and the past as behind.

Some examples in English:

I'm looking forward to the weekend.
They're looking ahead to next year.
He looked back over his life.
They don't foresee any problems.
The rest of your life is ahead of you.
Put the past behind you where it belongs.
Tuesday comes after Monday, and before Wednesday.

Time is treated like a path you are travelling along: as you walk along a path, the part of the path you have not reached yet is physically in front of you. The part of the path you have already walked along is physically behind you.

In some other cultures it's the opposite. The past is thought of as in front of us and the future as behind us. This might be hard to get your mind around because you have grown up using another metaphor to speak and think about time, but in some languages, '*ahead*' is a conventional metaphor for past, and '*behind*' for future. For example, in the Gurindji language (Northern Territory):

- kamparri-jang (*ahead/front*) means 'old, previous'
- ngumayi-jang (*behind*) means 'young(er), future'

This metaphor is difficult for us to understand but it makes sense to the Gurindji. It seems to be based on a scenario of travelling - those that are ahead have already been here; those behind have yet to reach here.

Taxonomies

Semantic Relations such as antonymy and synonymy refer to the relationships between the stored meanings of words in the lexicon.

There is another set of relations we have not looked at yet. The meanings of words group together into *lexical fields*. This is a little complex at first, but it is important to understand as it can be very different in different languages. Let's look at some examples: *Pig*, *cat*, *lion*, and *echidna* have meanings that relate to each other because they all belong to the same lexical field ('*animals*').

We are going to use some new terminology here so we can talk about lexical fields and the way they work. Don't worry about memorizing the specific terms - the main goal is for you to understand the concept of areas of meaning, and how they work. Basically words group together in different areas and levels of meaning. We will also be drawing diagrams to make it easier to understand.

The *superordinate* for *pig*, *cat*, *lion*, and *echidna* is 'animal'. Each term in a lexical field is a *hyponym* of the superordinate, so - *pig* is a hyponym of *animal*. The hyponyms of a single superordinate are *sisters* of each other, so - *pig*, *cat*, *lion*, and *echidna* are sisters.

A word can be a hyponym of one word, but the superordinate of another - *dog* is a hyponym of *animal*, but is itself the superordinate for *labrador*, *poodle*, *blue heeler*, etc.

As you can see, word meanings form complex hierarchical sets of relations called *taxonomies*. Here is an illustration of the one we have been talking about above:

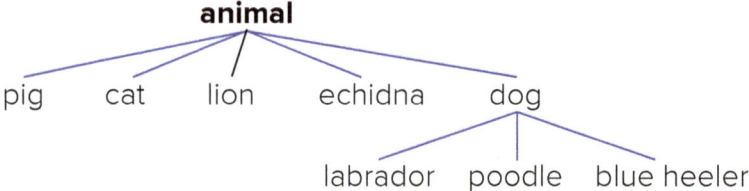

A single word can fit into several different taxonomies in different ways. For example, if we think of a distinction between humans and animals we might draw a taxonomy like this:

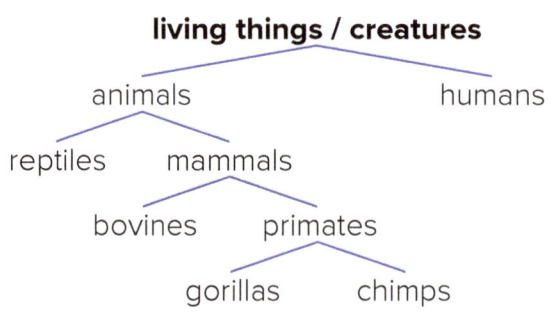

Those who make no distinction, might consider humans as a type of primate and would draw a different taxonomy:

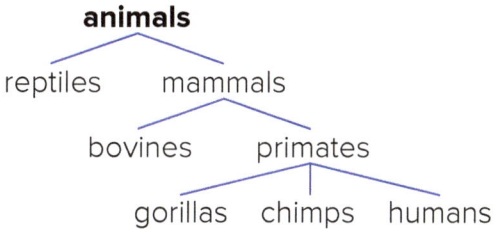

Taxonomies are cultural. Different cultures divide up the world differently. For example, in English, we would consider *bird* and *bat* to be separate taxonomies, with *chicken*, *pigeon* and *parrot* under the superordinate *bird*. But *fruit bat* and *vampire bat* we would not consider in that group. However in Kokota (Solomon Islands): *memeha* is the superordinate for the taxonomy that includes all of these:

kokorako *'chicken'*

balhu *'pigeon'*

makara *'parrot'*

meruku *'fruit bat'*

bablata *'insectivorous bat'*

ACTIVITIES

1. Are the following polysemy or homonymy?
   - bark (of a dog / of a tree)
   - steer (to guide / young bull)
   - fork (in road / instrument for eating)
   - lip (of jug / of person)
   - tail (of coat / of animal)
   - punch (fruity drink / blow)
   - mouse (on computer/animal)

SEMANTICS 1

2. Are the following examples of gradable antonyms? (A good test is to see if they can be combined with intensifiers such as very, very much, how, how much. If so, they are probably gradable antonyms.)
- big-small
- top-bottom
- long-short
- love-hate
- clever-stupid

3. Are the following complementary pairs?
- chalk-cheese
- dead-alive
- same-different
- married-unmarried
- copper-tin
- love-hate

4. Are these examples of relational opposites (converses)?
- below-above
- conceal-reveal
- grandparent-grandchild
- greater than-less than
- love-hate
- own-belong to

5. Describe as clearly as you can what the metaphors in the following verses mean.
- **PSALM 18:2** - *"The LORD is my rock, my fortress, and my savior; my God is my rock, in whom I find protection. He is my shield, the power that saves me, and my place of safety."*
- **JOHN 6:35** - *"Jesus replied, "I am the bread of life. Whoever comes to me will never be hungry again. Whoever believes in me will never be thirsty."*
- **JOHN 10:9** - *"Yes, I am the gate. Those who come in through me will be saved. They will come and go freely and will find good pastures."*
- **JAMES 3:6** - *"And the tongue is a flame of fire. It is a whole world of wickedness, corrupting your entire body. It can set your whole life on fire, for it is set on fire by hell itself.*

✓ **ANSWERS**

1. Polysemy or homonymy?
   - bark (of a dog / of a tree) **homonymy**
   - steer (to guide / young bull) **homonymy**
   - fork (in road / instrument for eating) **polysemy**
   - lip (of jug / of person) **polysemy**
   - tail (of coat / of animal) **polysemy**
   - punch (fruity drink / blow) **homonymy**
   - mouse (on computer / animal) **polysemy**
2. Gradable antonyms?
   - big-small **gradable**
   - top-bottom
   - long-short **gradable**
   - love-hate **gradable**
   - clever-stupid **gradable**
3. Complementary pairs?
   - chalk-cheese
   - dead-alive **complementary**
   - same-different **complementary**
   - married-unmarried **complementary**
   - copper-tin
   - love-hate (not complementary: just because you don't love something, you don't have to hate it)
4. Converses?
   - below-above **converses**
   - conceal-reveal
   - grandparent-grandchild **converses**
   - greater than-less than **converses**
   - love-hate
   - own-belong to **converses**

5. Describe as clearly as you can what the metaphors in the following verses mean.

Answers will vary. The metaphors used are describing something or someone in terms of another thing, and by doing so, are attributing properties or characteristics of that thing to the one they are describing:

- **PSALM 18:2**: The Lord is referred to as a rock, fortress and shield - all of these things have the properties of strength and being able to be a protection from danger. The Lord is an impenetrable barrier against spiritual harm and is able to stand up to any danger.
- **JOHN 6:35**: Jesus is referred to as the bread of life. The metaphor goes on to imply that only He can satisfy spiritual hunger and thirst, and that if He is the one to satisfy it, that it will not constantly return like physical hunger and thirst.
- **JOHN 10:9**: Jesus talks about Himself as the gate - referring to a gate of a sheepfold where a good shepherd would sleep to protect the sheep during the night. In this case He says He is the gate where people enter to be saved (through Him only can people be saved), and then that they can come and go freely to find good pasture (that people have true freedom once they are saved because of His perfect payment for their sin).
- **JAMES 3:6**: The metaphor uses fire because of the quality it has of getting out of control and running away from the person who thought they were controlling it. The warning is that people can think they are in control of the things they say, but if they are not careful and thoughtful, that the things they say can get out of control (be misunderstood or passed on by others and do great harm). Also, the things you say can bring harm to yourself also by ruining your life and thinking.

5.16 Semantics 2

OBJECTIVES OF THIS TUTORIAL

This tutorial continues to discuss Semantics. The last tutorial focused on the relationships between the meanings of words, but in this one we will look more specifically at sentences, and the implied meaning in sentences.

Introduction

As well as the meanings of individual words and expressions, semantics also involves the relationship between the meanings of sentences, and other pieces of meaning you might not actually be saying, but which might be implied in a sentence. A meaning that is asserted or implied in a sentence is called a *proposition*.

In this tutorial we will be discussing the relationship between propositions, and looking at some examples in English and in other languages.

Propositions

Propositions are always either true or false – we say that they have a truth-value. For example, *Sydney is a large city in Australia* is a proposition, and it has the truth-value of being true. Another proposition is: *Sydney is a city in Mexico*, and it has the truth-value of being false.

Some propositions have a meaning that requires that something *else* is also true or false - so if Proposition A is true, then Proposition B must also be true, and at the same time, if Proposition B is true, then Proposition A must also be true. For example,

> *That apple is in front of the oranges.*
> *Those oranges are behind the apple.*

If it's true that the apple is in front of the oranges, then it must also be true that the oranges are behind the apple. To say that the oranges are behind the apple entails that

153

the apple is in front of them, and vice versa. We call this *entailment* - it describes the relationship between these kinds of propositions.

Sometimes the entailment only works one way - for example:

>*I own a dog.*

>*I own a pet.*

If Proposition A is true, then Proposition B must also be true, but if Proposition B is true, that doesn't necessarily mean that Proposition A is also true. To say I own a dog entails that I own a pet, but to say that I own a pet does not entail that I own a dog - my pet might be an anaconda or a kitten.

Entailment is just one way in which propositions relate to one another in their meaning. Let's look at another meaning relationship that involves propositions.

Presupposition

Think about the following proposition:

>*The Prime Minister of Australia in 2012 was a woman.*

It is easy to determine the truth-value of this proposition – it's true. But what about:

>*The King of New Zealand in 2012 was of Maori heritage.*

We say that this proposition has no truth-value – it's neither true nor false - because it is based on a *presupposition* that isn't valid.

The proposition about the Australian Prime Minister has truth-value because there *was* an Australian Prime Minister in 2012 - so we say it has a valid presupposition. But the proposition about the New Zealand King has no truth-value - it is based on a presupposition that is not valid - because there's no position of 'King of New Zealand', not yet anyway.

Each of these propositions involves a *presupposition*. To say *the New Zealand King is Maori* presupposes that there is a New Zealand King. If we say it's true, we are also accepting that there is a New Zealand King, but if we say it's false, we're still accepting that there's a New Zealand King (but that he's of some other ethnicity). So, to say the New Zealand King is *not* Maori presupposes there is a New Zealand King, just as much as the positive proposition.

So, statements can have presuppositions - but other sentence types like questions can also. For example: *Do you like the current King of New Zealand?*

You can't answer yes or no, because the question involves the presupposition that there is a current NZ king, and that presupposition is not valid.

Presuppositions are very powerful. Lawyers in court are supposed to be careful not to ask people questions that have dangerous presuppositions, like;

Have you stopped forging your employer's signature?

If you answer yes, you are accepting the presupposition that you used to forge your employer's signature, but if you answer no, you are admitting you are still doing it!

Context

It is probably an obvious thing to say, because we all know that a lot of the meaning in words and sentences depends on the *context* of the things being said. If someone says to you;

"Find out first and then come back tomorrow, and buy another one of those."

What are you supposed to find out? Where are you meant to come back to? When? And what are you supposed to buy? The only way you can understand that sentence is if you know the context - who is speaking, what they are talking about, etc.

To understand the meaning of a lot of sentences you need to know about the speech event - the event of the words themselves being said. Linguists call this kind of meaning *deixis* - which is simply the meaning that depends on knowledge of the time and place and participants in the speech event.

There are three main kinds of information about context that are important to the meaning of speech: *the personal context*, *the physical context* and *the time context*. The *social context* also is important to meaning. We will look at some of the things in language that indicate personal information first.

The Personal Context

Person and number

To understand the meaning of what someone is saying, one of the first things you need to know is who the speaker is and also who they are talking about. Pronouns are the main way that this personal context is made clear.

Pronouns distinguish categories of *person*, and usually also of *number*:

- First person refers to the speaker or any group including the speaker.
- Second person refers to the addressee or a group including the addressee.
- Third person refers to anyone or anything not including the speaker and/or addressee.

SEMANTICS 2

In English we have three *person* categories and two *number* categories (except in second person where there is no number because there is no singular and plural):

	First Person	Second Person	Third Person		
			Masculine	*Feminine*	*Neutral*
Singular	I, me, my, mine	you, your, yours	he, him, his	she, her, hers	it, its, their
Plural	we, us, our, ours		they, them, their, theirs		

It is important to know that many languages don't work the same way as English in person and number - how they communicate who is talking and who they are talking about.

A lot of languages have *four person categories*, because they have an extra first person category. They have one first person category that includes the speaker and others but *not* the person they are talking to (first person exclusive) and another one that includes the speaker and others *as well as* the person they are talking to (first person inclusive).

English doesn't make this distinction, so when someone says to you, "We are going to the beach", they could mean that the trip to the beach includes you - the person they are talking to - or they might be talking about a group that doesn't include you. The *we* in English doesn't make it clear. However in the Wajarri (Aboriginal, Western Australia) language, you would always know if you were included in the beach trip or not because the speaker can indicate that by the pronoun he uses (first person inclusive or exclusive):

	First Person (Inclusive)	First Person (Exclusive)	Second Person	Third Person
Singular	ŋaja	—	nyinta	palu
Dual	ŋali	ŋalija	nyupali	pula
Plural	ŋanyu	ŋanju	nyurra	jana

You may have noticed that Wajarri also has an extra *number* category as well - Dual. The dual number category shows they are talking about two people - many languages have this dual category. Some languages also distinguish *trial* (three), or *paucal* (a few - more than two but not many) in their pronouns.

Standard Fijian uses four person categories and four number categories:

	First Person (Inclusive)	First Person (Exclusive)	Second Person	Third Person
Singular	yau	—	iko	koya
Dual	keirau	kedatu	kemudrau	rau
Paucal	keitou	kedatou	kemudou	iratou
Plural	keimami	keda	kemuni	ira

Case and Gender

Pronouns can also distinguish *case* - which indicates if the person being spoken about is the subject or the object of the sentence. They can also distinguish *gender* - masculine or feminine.

In English "*I*" is the first person singular pronoun if the speaker is the *subject* of the sentence, but we use "*me*" (still first person singular) if the speaker is the *object*; and we use "*mine*" (also first person singular) if the speaker is the possessor. This ability of English pronouns to distinguish in this way is called *case*. Not all languages have case - many just use the same pronouns regardless of case, like Fijian.

You would have seen in the table of English pronouns above, that we distinguish three categories of *gender*, but only in third person singular - masculine, feminine and neutral. French only distinguishes two gender categories, and again only in third person singular. Some languages distinguish gender in other person or number categories as well. For example, Arabic also distinguishes gender in second person singular, second person plural and third person plural.

As we have seen, all languages use pronouns to make it clear who is speaking and whom they are speaking about - but they work in different ways to communicate this personal context. Next we will see how languages indicate other important information about the context of what is being said.

The Physical Context

There are indicators in languages that help to locate an event or object in physical space and we will be looking at some examples of these below. The actual speech context - where the thing is being said - also adds to the *physical context* of a sentence.

SEMANTICS 2

Directional verbs

Some verbs of motion have locative meanings. *Come* means, 'move towards the location where the word *come* is uttered'. *Go* means, 'move away from a location' - the default location is the location where the word *go* is uttered.

Spatial adverbs

There are also locative adverbs (adverbs of location) that tell us things about physical location. *Here*, refers to a location near the place where it is uttered. *There*, refers to a location away from the place where it is uttered. Many languages have more locative adverbs than English. Some examples are Southern Sotho (Niger-Congo) which distinguishes degrees of distance with its locative adverbs.

'here' (near the speech event)	'there' (a little way away from the speech event)	'there' (a long way away from the speech event)
seē	seō	sanē

Japanese has three types of locative adverbs that relate to the person speaking and also to the personal context:

'here' (near the speaker: 1st person)	'there' (near the one being spoken to: 2nd person)	'there' (away from the speech event: 3rd person)
koko	soko	ano

Some languages distinguish many more than three categories of distance. Some combine both distance-based and person-based dimensions, like Hausa (Afro-Asiatic):

'here' (near the speaker)	'there' (near the one being spoken to)	'there' (a little away from the speech event)	'there' (a long way away from the speech event)
nân	nan	cân	can

Other languages have much more complex systems that include elements of relative height; relationship to directions of rivers or locations of coastlines; movement away from or towards; and other factors. The Ata language (spoken by people who live along narrow river valleys in the mountains of PNG) commonly uses the locative adverbs - *to'o* and *nuna* ('upstream' and 'downstream'), relating the direction to the flow of the river which is a constant reference point in their world.

Demonstratives

Demonstratives refer to things and where they are in relation to the location of speaking - we have two demonstrative categories in English:

	(near the speech event)	(away from the speech event)
Singular	'this'	'that'
Plural	'these'	'those'

Some languages distinguish more demonstrative categories, like Tlingit (Alaska):

'this' (near the speaker)	'that' (near the addressee)	'that' (a little way away)	'that' (a long way away)
yaa	hei	wee	yoo

Other languages have *even more* categories, like Kokota (Oceanic, Solomon Islands) which has five distance categories:

	'this' (touching)	'this' (within reach)	'that' (nearby)	'that' (visible)	'that' (not visible)
Singular	ao	ine	ana	iao	-o
Plural	aro	ide	are	iaro	-ro

The Social Context

Some languages have ways of expressing a relationship with the speaker that is not in space or in time, but in society. For example, some European languages have second person pronouns that distinguish social distance from the speaker. In German, the more familiar way to say 'you' is *du* (singular) or *ihr* (plural). However, if you are being more polite or formal you would use *Sie* (both singular and plural).

Some East Asian languages express the complex social hierarchies that exist in those cultures. For example, Javanese (Austronesian, Java) has different first person singular and second person singular pronouns depending on whether the speaker is higher in the social hierarchy than the addressee, or on the same level, or lower:

Addressee is:	First person singular	Second person singular
much higher	daləm	pandzənə'an
a bit higher	kulo	sampejan
not higher	aku	kowe

SEMANTICS 2

The way these terms interact is very complex. Javanese social distance requires the use of many completely different words for the same meaning - depending on their social status compared to the speaker. This feature of the language reflects the great importance that is placed on social status in the Javanese culture.

The Time Context

There are words and phrases that we use to locate events in *time*, in relation to the moment of the speech event. Some of these in English are:

- *now* means roughly at the time the word *now* is said,
- *then* means at a time other than when the word *then* is said,
- *tomorrow* means the day following the day when the word *tomorrow* is said;
- *last week* means the week before the week during which the phrase is said.

Tense

You have probably heard of tense - it is a grammatical system of locating events in time in relation to the moment of speaking. *Past tense*, like in the word 'walked', locates the event of walking some time before the moment of speaking.

Different languages differ quite a bit in the way they express tense. Many languages (like Fijian and Hindi), have three tenses, *past*, *present* and *future* - but some languages have no tense system at all, like Thai and Vietnamese. Many languages have only two tenses - if a language has only two tenses it almost always distinguishes *past* vs. *non-past*. Japanese is a language with two tenses.

Many languages have more than one past tense. Some languages have more than one future tense. An interesting fact is that languages *never* have more future tenses than past tenses.

Some languages distinguish many tenses. For example, Rotokas (Bougainville) has four past tenses and two future tenses:

Aio-ri-va.	'You ate (long ago).'	*remote past*
Aio-ri-vora.	'You ate (some time ago).'	*distant past*
Aio-ri-vorao.	'You ate (not long ago).'	*near past*
Aio-ri-vo.	'You ate (just now).'	*immediate past*
Aio-ri-voi.	'You are eating.'	*present*
Aio-ri-vere.	'You will eat (soon).'	*near future*
Aio-ri-verea.	'You will eat (a long time from now).'	*distant future*

Tense in English

Many people agree that English has only two tenses: past and non-past (like Japanese). Past is marked with a past tense marker, the suffix *–ed* (walk, walked). Non-past is unmarked - there are no separate present and future tenses in English.

The auxiliary word *will,* often functions like a future tense marker. But often when we are talking of the future, we do not use *will*, but use another auxiliary word instead:

> He *will* arrive tomorrow.
>
> He *might* arrive tomorrow.
>
> He *should* arrive tomorrow.
>
> He *can* arrive tomorrow.

Many future references even use the simple non-past:

> He*'s* arriving tomorrow.
>
> He arrive*s* tomorrow.

 ACTIVITIES

1. The following sentences have certain presuppositions, even if the situation isn't completely known. What are they?
- Frank saw the horse with two heads.
- Johannes Piper died in misery.
- Stephanie began planting trees.
- What Jan lost wasn't her handbag.
- Even Claudio could solve that problem.

2. For each of the sentences below (marked A), state which of the accompanying statements (marked B) show entailment (i.e., if A is true, then B must be true).

A: Mr Green stole the Mona Lisa this morning.
   B: Mr Green stole something.
   B: Something was stolen this morning.
   B: Mr Green believes the Mona Lisa is valuable.

A: Who stole the Mona Lisa this morning?
   B: Mr Green stole something.
   B: Something was stolen this morning.

ANSWER

1. Presuppositions:

Remember that presuppositions are things that are assumed by the speaker to be already known to the addressee.

- Frank saw the horse with two heads >> There exists a horse with two heads.
- Johannes Piper died in misery >> There is some individual named Johannes Piper.
- Stephanie began planting trees >> Stephanie had not been planting trees before.
- What Jan lost wasn't her handbag >> Jan lost something.
- Even Claudio could solve that problem >> Claudio is the last person you'd expect to be able to solve the problem.

2. Entailment:

  A: Mr Green stole the Mona Lisa this morning.

   B: Mr Green stole something. **Yes**

   B: Something was stolen this morning. **Yes**

   B: Mr Green believes the Mona Lisa is valuable. **No**

  A: Who stole the Mona Lisa this morning?

   B: Mr Green stole something. **No**

   B: Something was stolen this morning. **Yes**

5.17 Pragmatics

OBJECTIVES OF THIS TUTORIAL

This tutorial looks at - pragmatics - or language in use. Pragmatics is what we do with our language -how we indicate what we want, what we think and what we need. It is where all the other linguistic areas we have looked at so far come together to make communication happen.

Introduction

When we acquire our first language we learn the sounds of the language, as well as the principles of the phonology and syntax. But this is not enough. We also learn how to *use* the language.

When we are children we quickly learn how to make requests, later we learn how to issue invitations, give orders, ask for information and greet and farewell people in socially appropriate ways. As well as learning how to do these things, we also learn how to interpret them correctly.

Pragmatics looks at meaning in context, and why a speaker chose to speak in exactly the way they did.

Speech acts

When we ask questions, issue invitations, give orders, ask for information or greet and farewell people, we are actually performing an action by saying something - a speech act. Everything we say is made up of a series of one or more speech acts.

There are different types of speech act:

Direct**ives**

This is when the speaker is trying to get someone else to do something, e.g.:

    Requests - *"Would you mind passing the salt?"*

    Commands - *"Pass the salt!"*

    Begging - *"Please, please pass the salt."*

    Questions - *"Where is the salt?"*

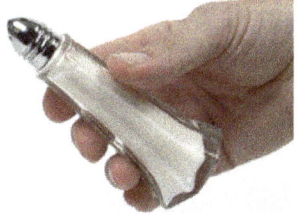

Commissives

The speaker is committing himself or herself to doing something in the future:

> Promises - *"I'll pay it back to you by Thursday."*
> Guarantees - *"You can count on me to pay it back."*
> Threats - *"I'll have to report you if you do that again."*
> Offers - *"I'll go to the shop on the way home if you like."*

Expressives

The speaker is expressing their feelings or attitude, e.g.:

> Apologies - *"I'm sorry I left you alone."*
> Sympathising - *"I hope you are going to be OK."*
> Welcoming - *"Please come in and make yourself at home."*
> Thanks - *"Thanks for bringing that back."*
> Congratulations - *"That's great news you won the trip!"*

Representatives

The speaker is giving information – they are making a claim about whether a proposition is true or not, e.g.:

> Predictions - *"It's going to be hot today."*
> Claims - *"I think it's hot today."*
> Assertions - *"It's hot outside."*
> Hypothesising - *"It feels like it could be hot later today."*
> Conclusions - *"It must be hot outside."*

Declarations

The speaker changes something in the world by the act of speaking, e.g.:

> Resigning - *"I quit."*
> Naming - *"We'll call him Sam."*
> Marrying - *"I now pronounce you man and wife."*
> Hiring - *"You've got the job, you start on Monday."*
> Firing - *"You should start looking for a position that is a better fit for your skill set."*

Common Ground

No matter which of these types of speech act someone is performing, we need to consider the meaning *in context*, to figure out why the speaker chose to speak in exactly the way they did and what they intended to mean. Look at the last example from above -

"You should start looking for a position that is a better fit for your skill set."

Because you were given the information that this statement is an example of 'firing' - you probably imagined a scene where an employer was gently letting his employee know that he was being fired. But, if you were not given that clue to the context, the statement *could* be interpreted in many different ways. It might be someone giving advice to a friend, or a rival employer trying to convince this person to leave their current job and join their staff instead, or it might be a mother protecting her child from disappointment after they had been corrected at work, or it could even be a golf coach helping his client who has a bad swing.

So, in order to interpret statements correctly, we need to be able to draw on *common ground*. The common ground needed to correctly interpret the statement above would include all of these kinds of things:

- who is speaking
- who they are speaking to
- all you know about these people - their personalities, status, gender, their relationship to one another
- the interactional history between them (e.g. is this an employee the boss has been struggling with for years? Is it his favorite nephew? etc.)
- information about how the world works which is reasonably widely known within the culture (e.g. an understanding that jobs are highly sought after, that a business can't keep on unproductive employees, that people have to sell their skills to employers, etc.)

In other words, common ground is the sort of assumed knowledge that speakers bring to a conversation. It is the reason that when a man tells the story about how he lost his job and now doesn't have the money to pay the mortgage this month, it would be told in quite a different way to his bank manager, than to his sister (with whom he shares a much greater degree of common ground).

Good language learning programs say that culture and language are inseparable, and that before someone is able to communicate clearly in a cross-cultural situation, they need to learn both the culture and the language. Another way of putting this is that people need to learn, not just to *speak* the language but how to *use* the language. Their ability to really use the language is based on this aspect of sharing *common ground*. They need to develop an understanding of culture, including how relationships work, information about how the world works and how people interact - and they also need to have real relationships with people, so that they can speak into those relationships based on a shared life experience and mutual understanding.

Intended meaning

Even with shared common ground, it is not always clear what someone intends to mean by what they say. Even between two native speakers, there is often a difference between the speaker's intended meaning and the meaning that the hearer understands from what they heard. So linguists distinguish between the *illocution* (what the speaker intended) and *perlocution* (what the hearer understood) of an utterance.

If someone says to me: "You did a great job this time!" - their intended meaning could be that they really appreciated the work I did, but if I am insecure for some reason, I may hear them to be saying that I did a terrible job last time.

Because illocution is open to interpretation, speakers will sometimes use it in quite subtle ways. We have all heard people make critical remarks but then deny that they meant the comment to be offensive (e.g., "She's looking slimmer today.") We are also familiar with the way politicians use ambiguous words and phrases so that they can deny the real meaning of their remarks at a later time.

In spoken language, we can often use the tone of our voice, or stress on particular words, or gestures and facial expressions to convey what our meaning is. If the example from above was spoken by a friend with a smile on their face and stress on the word *great* (You did a *great job* this time!), then their intended meaning is much clearer. If it was said by a critical person with an angry expression on their face and different stress (You did a great job *this* time!), I would be likely to interpret it as a criticism rather than praise.

Cooperation in conversation

So far we have looked at individual speech acts. But how do participants in a conversation structure and interpret utterances in light of what has gone before?

There are general rules that we follow when we have

a conversation - we cooperate together to make the conversation 'work'. Not everyone always follows these rules, but people who obey the cooperative principle in their language use will make sure that what they say in a conversation furthers the *purpose* of that particular conversation. The cooperative principle has been broken down (by Grice 1975:45-6) into these 'rules' for good conversation:

1. Make your contribution to the conversation as informative as necessary.
2. Do not make your contribution to the conversation *more* informative than necessary.
3. Do not say what you believe to be false.
4. Do not say anything for which you lack adequate evidence
5. Be relevant (i.e., say things related to the current topic of the conversation).
6. Avoid obscurity of expression (use words the other person will understand).
7. Avoid ambiguity (be clear in what you say).
8. Be brief (avoid unnecessary wordiness).
9. Be orderly.

These rules are about how a good speaker should behave in conversation for the conversation to achieve its purpose. People sometimes lie, give too much information, exaggerate, etc. so it is clear that not all people obey the cooperative principle at all times.

It can also seem that many everyday utterances also seem to break the rules too:

> A: *Do you know what time it is?*
> B: *Yeah, I know, I'm nearly ready!*
> *The new smart phone is like, a million times better!*
> *Yeah, the earth is flat, pigs can fly and Henry will be here on time.*

All of the statements above seem to break either the rule of relevance or truthfulness. But in reality, these utterances are not uncooperative; they just should not be taken literally. They are indirect speech acts, and so we need to look at what message a speaker *implies* in what they are saying:

> In the first one, A was giving B a subtle hurry up.
> The second one implies the new phone is much, much better.
> The third one is implying that I doubt Henry will come on time.

Indirectness

In all of these examples, the speaker is not saying exactly what they mean. Not saying what we mean might seem to make communication more difficult, but it actually serves a number of functions. The biggest advantage of using implication is that it allows us to be much briefer in what we say than if we spelt out exactly what we meant. In fact, people who know each other well can often rely on shared background knowledge to an extraordinary degree.

Indirect statements are also used in order to appear more polite. We rely on our knowledge of implication to interpret statements such as, *"Wow, it's quite warm in here, isn't it?"* as a request to open a window. The thinking process I might go through if someone said that to me while visiting our home is something like:

1. People do not make statements for no reason.
2. Why is she sharing this statement with me?
3. Ah, she must want me to do something about it.

Why is it that indirectness is seen to aid politeness? The answer lies in the *freedom* it gives the hearer in acting upon the request. Any request is a potentially face-threatening act, as it imposes on the hearer's freedom to act as they please.

If my visitor says to me straight out *"Open the window"* or, *"I want you to open the window"* then I have to do it or risk starting an argument. If, however, they are less direct and say, *"It's warm in here, isn't it?"* then it gives me an easy way out if I don't want to open the window – I can simply agree with my visitor and the situation is dealt with. I don't look rude for not complying and they don't look like they're being bossy.

As we already saw when we looked at some of the differences between cultures, some cultures value freedom and individuality more than others, and some cultures are much more indirect than others. Unless you are aware of the differences that can exist between cultures in these kinds of areas, there can easily be hurt feelings and misunderstandings - *"Oh, these people are so impolite!"*

Direct and indirect language

The function of a speech act may differ from the sentence type of the utterance. For example;

- *"I'd like a drink"*, has the form of a statement, but the intended speech act is actually a request.
- *"Can you shut the door?"* has the form of a question, but the intended speech act is a command.

Interrogatives (questions) in English are often used for functions other than questions. They are often used for commands as well - *"Would you mind shutting the door?"* or *"Can I ask you to shut the door please?"* They can also be used for suggestions - *"Should we stay for another drink?"* or invitations - *"Why don't you come over for dinner tomorrow?"*

Declaratives can also be used for commands - *"That's my coat behind you"* (meaning "Pass me my coat which is behind you."), or invitations - *"You're welcome to join us for dinner tomorrow"*, or warnings - *"You're driving too fast."*

When the *intended function* of an utterance matches its *sentence type* we say that it is a **direct speech act**. *"Can you drive a car?"* is a direct speech act; it has the form of an interrogative, with the 'normal' function of a question – a request for information.

When the function and sentence type *do not* match, it is an **indirect speech act**. *"Do you know what the time is?"* has the form of a question, but it would not (normally) be used as a yes-no question; its normal function would be a request for action, for the hearer to tell you the time, or even for the hearer to hurry up and get ready. So it serves the indirect speech act of a request. *"What are you looking at?"* could be a genuine request for information (direct speech act: question) or it could have the indirect speech act of a threat or warning (stop looking at me).

Cultural diversity in speech acts

Just as the phonology, morphology and syntax of each language is different, the way utterances are used to perform acts differs from language to language.

In many languages, including English, there are special words for greeting and fare welling such as *hello* and *goodbye*. Neither of these mean anything else. However, in English we also use phrases or sentences that seem to mean something else as greetings or farewells: *"How are you?"* or *"How's it going?"* These sentences are not normally intended as a request for information. *"See you later"*, is a reduced version of a statement. *"Take care"*, and *"Have a nice day"*, have the sentence form of a command, but are not normally intended to be commands, but leave-takings.

Expressions that other languages use for greetings vary in their sentence type and function as well:

The Dowayo (Cameroon) greet each other using a sentence meaning "Is the sky clear for you?" This is a sentence of the interrogative type, but is not a request for information. The Kokota (Solomon Islands) greet each other with *lao hai* "Where are you going?" but are astonished and amused if the addressee actually attempts to give them an informative answer. And the Naxi (southern China) greet one another by saying *a lala le* - "Are your arms busy?" (meaning, "Are you feeling well enough to be busy working?")

Farewell sequences also differ cross-linguistically. In almost every culture, it isn't normal for people to simply walk away when they take their leave, they will almost always utter a formulaic farewell statement.

In many languages the farewell has the sentence type of a command. In some it means "stay here" - as in Ata (PNG), where the most common leave-taking is to say *nini naxolu, eni alai* "You stay, I will go". In Fijian they say *moce*, "sleep!" These are not interpreted as instructions to not leave after the speaker has left, or to go to sleep, they are simply farewells.

Languages also differ in the relationship between speech act and sentence type. For example, in English, commands are not usually given using imperative or direct statements. In other cultures commands are usually given with direct statements, and an interrogative would not be interpreted as a command. So in English, if a passenger wants a bus driver to open the door of a bus, he would normally say something like "*Could you open the door please?*", but in Hebrew, the normal form would be "*Open the door.*"

DISCUSSION POINTS

1. Below is a historical story (from the 1980s), written by a member of the Ata people group (New Britain, PNG). Read the English translation and try to figure out what the story is about and what is happening in the story. On the next page is a clear explanation. What are some of the misunderstandings that arose when you just read the translation of the story below and what are the specific pieces of shared knowledge you were missing? What does this illustrate in terms of cross-cultural communication?

Molomolo laposalaxu (in Ata language)

Loxo molomolo laposalaxu io ulai no taoni la nenu ilou momu i'oxonu la'ilali. Loxo ane'i i'oxonu la'ilali la ilalaxinu la'ilali ane. Imolo sie mo ia'asou toto'o mo ia'asou mo'u mo ia'asou sikapu mo ixeta'u ue. Ilalaxinu la'ilali ane xe ixalixu no tuala ukalu laso ane'i tatulanu molomolo ne ino'u so ilaixu no taoni. Ilaixu no taoni la ane'i tasema no tuala mo tamulu no tuala ne tasema so ixa'umusou la'ilali xe tamulu so itelaiou ualu. Ukalu xe anu so o'olovoxo la ane'i tamitema no tuala ilalaxi so ikuakua.

Loxo ane'i ilalaxi la ilalaxinu mi loxo tavi mo lapoe mo lavo'o. Xe ivisime'a ane'i no taoni xe ixali la ane'i tamitema no tuala ive'a ane'i ane milaixu molomolo no taoni ne. Ane'i ive'a ive'a xo xe ukalu. Laso ane'i ilaixu molomolo no tani. Xe olovoxo laso ane'i ilalaxi so ixumu no olovoxo. Loxo ane'i ixumu la tasema ilei no ale xe tamulu so ilei nonano.

The First-born Child (translation of the Ata story above)

If a child is the first-born child, and he goes to town, then his mother and father would prepare some food. They would prepare the food like this: they would gather taro and dig up sweet potato and dig up yams and dig up sikapu [another root vegetable], and they would cut sugar cane. Once they had gathered the food and then carried it back to the village, then they would get ready to go with the child to take him to town. They would take him to town, but meanwhile the women in the village and the men in the village would ixa'umusou food [cook food by burying it under hot stones]. Then the men would climb coconut trees. Later on, toward evening, the people in the village would get ready to ikuakua [call out from the ridge].

They would get ready like that, and they would also prepare spears and stone axes and rocks. Then they would wait for the people to come back from town. When they arrived, then the people in the village would hit them; the people with the child who had been to town. They would hit them, and hit them, and then it would be finished, and then they would take the child into the house. Then that night, they would get ready to eat the food they had prepared. They would all eat the food, and the women would dance outside the house, and the men would dance inside.

ACTIVITIES

1. For each of the following utterances, state the possible intended meaning and any possible interpretations;
  a. I don't suppose you could spare five dollars.
  b. It's a bit cold in here.
  c. Are you doing anything special tomorrow night?
  d. That dog bites.
  e. You're not going out looking like that, young lady!
  f. I'd love another slice of chocolate cake, you're so kind.
  g. Walk and talk!
  h. Why is there chocolate all over the couch?

2. Rephrase each of the utterances above as direct speech acts - where someone says exactly what they mean rather than implying it.

The First-born Child (Further explanation)

In Ata culture, the first-born child of a family has an important role in the family and a higher status in the village and clan than subsequent children, so the people of their village celebrate any significant event in the first-born child's life. The child's first trip to town is significant, because in a mountain village, making a trip to town was a relatively rare event. The foods mentioned would only be all eaten together for a special event, because it would be quite extravagant to eat all of these together - and the addition of sugar cane and the mention of the men climbing coconut trees (the implication being that they are gathering coconuts to eat) also marks this event as being a special event and an important feast.

Calling out from the ridge (*ikuakua*) is a traditional yodeling welcome cry that is unique to the Ata mountain people. A group returning to the village would call out from a long distance to their family in the village on the high ridges, who would then reply with the same cry. This is done to let them know they are on their way back to the village after a long trip away, so the people in the village can prepare for their return. Hospitality is extremely important, and was often a matter of survival in the previous generations, when neighbouring tribes were at war with the Ata, or someone returning might have been in real need of food and shelter.

When the first-born child and his parents would return to the village, the people gathered there would "play act" hitting them with stones and axes and also thrusting spears in their direction, yelling at them and running toward them. This is a traditional way of greeting people at a significant event - such as when outsiders first come to the village, or when someone special returns after a long time away. Often the older women will also gather dirt from the ground or ash from the fire and cover their heads and faces with this dust as a sign of welcome. [There are historical and spiritual reasons for this behavior, which we won't explain in any more detail here].

The house that they would have taken the male child into is the *novi* or men's house. Traditionally women were not allowed into this house, so they would dance outside while the men would dance inside the men's house. The dancing would traditionally continue till dawn of the next day, and was a part of any significant event because every such event would have spiritual connotations as well as social ones, and dancing and singing had a spiritual function.

This 'first trip to town' is an important event in the life of the first-born child and his family, and so the Ata person recalling this decided to tell it as a significant story in their history and have it recorded in writing.

✓ ANSWERS

1. & 2. Possible intended meaning and any possible interpretations, and statements rephrased as direct speech acts:

   a. I don't suppose you could spare five dollars. (I want to borrow five dollars.)
   b. It's a bit cold in here. (Do something to make it warmer in here.)
   c. Are you doing anything special tomorrow night? (I want to make an arrangement with you for tomorrow night.)
   d. That dog bites. (Don't go near that dog/I think you should stay away from that dog.)
   e. You're not going out looking like that, young lady! (I don't approve of what you are wearing/I think what you are wearing is immodest.)
   f. I'd love another slice of chocolate cake, you're so kind. (You should have offered me another slice of chocolate cake.)
   g. Walk and talk! (I don't have time to stop and talk to you. I am more important than you, so hurry up and say what you have to say - I'm busy.)
   h. Why is there chocolate all over the couch? (I think you put chocolate all over the couch.)

5.18 Language and Identity

OBJECTIVES OF THIS TUTORIAL

This tutorial looks at the relationship between language and identity. People have strong feelings about their language, and it is often linked to various other parts of their identity, such as their nation, ethnic group, religion and social class.

Introduction

For those of us who come from a monolingual, English speaking background, language doesn't form a very conscious part of our identity. We don't think about the fact that we speak English (or a variety of English) very often. But for many people in the world, language is a very important part of their view of who they are. There are many multilingual communities around the world, where three or more languages are spoken by most people. In that situation, a person's primary language is a defining element of their personal identity and how others view them.

People have strong feelings about language, which is why there are numerous political battles involving language around the world. In many regions, smaller language groups are being 'absorbed' by larger languages/cultures around them. Some people groups, such as the Maori in New Zealand, have made an intense and very effective effort to make their language relevant and significant to younger generations of both Maori and non-Maori New Zealanders, because they see it as a key part of their identity as a people.

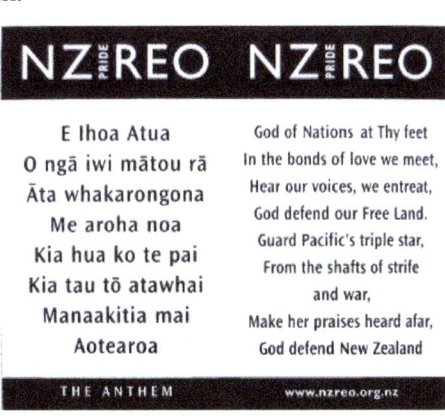

Our goal here is to discuss only some of the issues involved in the relationship between language and identity. It is a huge subject and one that many books have been written about. We will simply introduce some of the main ideas about the place that language has in the identity of a group and how it relates to other parts of their identity such as their ethnic group, nation, history, culture, and religion. Thinking about language and identity should improve our view of who we are, in our eyes and in other people's, and it should deepen our understanding of social interaction.

What is 'Identity'?

One way identity is sometimes defined is by categorising people according to various criteria – ethnic origin, language, national origin, etc. But we are going to look at it from the point of view of *how people view themselves*, and particularly how their language relates to the view they have of themselves.

Most definitions of identity agree that it is something like: *an individual person feeling they are a part of a group*. That feeling is based on them sharing certain values with others in the group, and finding a sense of belonging there:

> "Self-identification commonly involves identifying with a specific group or community based on a range of criteria: racial, ethnic, cultural, social, etc.; self-identification necessarily involves imposing boundaries between groups and emphasising one's belonging to one group rather than another; belonging to one group usually entails exclusion from another; self-identification also commonly involves emphasising sameness or similarities between the individual and the group he self-identifies with on the one hand, and emphasising the differences with other groups." (Rittner)

Some other descriptions that might help us to form a picture of what a identity is:
- a person recognises himself as a member of one or more groups
- the person shares values and meanings associated with a group
- a person recognises characteristics that they have in common with other members
- the person distinguishes himself from other people who do not share the group characteristics
- other members of the group recognise him as a member
- a group must see itself, and also be seen by other groups and individuals, as a distinct social entity
- some characteristics of the group may be thought of as more important than others - (core values or qualities)
- important characteristics or core values can differ depending on the situation: a characteristic becomes important if it can be seen as making a certain group distinct from other groups (skin color can be important in a multiracial society, while language can be an important feature in a multi-ethnic and multicultural society)

Self identity and Group identity

In Western, 'global' cultures the relationship between individual identity and group identity is very complex and diverse. A person's deep, personal identity is made up mostly by the various group identities they also have. So, someone who identifies himself as 'an Australian' may have an individual identity that includes being from a family of Chinese ethnic origin, belonging to the medical profession, being a part of a local Chinese speaking church, being able to speak two or more languages, and belonging to a group that plays guitar on the weekends. There would be many other people who identify as 'Australians' who do not share many, or even any, specific aspects of his individual identity with him. So is 'Australian-ness' a meaningful identity?

In a broad and complex global culture, group identity *is* a very abstract concept, but it is interesting to note that people still display a strong need to self-identify with a particular group:

> "...it would appear logical that in the increasingly globalised world we live in, with its ever increasing levels of communi cation, and with the decreasing importance of state and geographical boundaries, this need for identifying with a particular group or place will gradually grow weaker. As it turns out, the opposite seems to be the case - it seems that with the disappearance of borders and boundaries and geographical distances, this need for identity grows stronger, and with the diminished significance of boundaries individuals look for other salient features that will help them establish a sense of belonging to a particular group; in this language continues to play a huge role.." (Gibbons & Holt)

There are also many people groups in the world who are not greatly connected to the wider global culture, and who consequently have a much more concrete group identity which is tied in a large way to the unique languages they speak. They often have a cohesive view of who they are as a people group, and as individuals they find a much greater sense of belonging in their ethno-linguistic identity. For example, a person who calls himself an 'Ata' person (a people group in Papua New Guinea) would share a great number of individual identities with any other person who also calls themselves 'Ata'. But even for these types of people groups, in today's world there are often pressures from 'outside' that have the potential to threaten or confuse their sense of identity - or in some cases to change it completely. Sometimes these are positive influences and sometimes not, but no matter how it turns out, the process of change in identity as a people group is often a stressful and challenging one.

Above: Ata children learning to read and write their language.

Language and Identity

Anyone who writes about identity points out that while there are many aspects of a person's identity and many factors that can determine a person's identity - like ethnic, social or racial origin, culture, religion, education, professional occupation, family background, etc. - *language* is probably the most powerful instrument for constructing and expressing identity. People who speak the same heart language obviously have a much greater degree of shared common ground, common understanding and have the ability to develop a deeper relationship, so it follows that shared language is a primary way people identify with others. It is also a primary separating force between different groups.

Even *within* the same language community, we still use language to further identify a person. When we listen to someone speaking we are unconsciously evaluating and trying to identify 'who they are'. Do they have an accent? Are they from the city or the country? Are they well educated? Do they use certain words and not others? Speech is a very powerful factor in this identification process. When someone is talking, we are making social, cultural, and ethnic categorisations and value judgments based on their linguistic behavior. All of the levels of language (phonology, syntax, semantics, pragmatics) affect our beliefs about, and evaluation of, the speaker.

We use language to exchange meaningful (and sometimes very complex and subtle) messages with other members of the same linguistic community, but we are also using language to tell the rest of the world about ourselves - to mark ourselves as similar to or different from other individuals, to show which group we belong to, or which we would like to belong to.

Speech adjustment and identity

Speakers often make adjustments to their speech depending on who it is they are talking to - two of these types of adjustment are:

- *convergence* - speakers modify their speech in a way to make it more similar to the speech of the person they are speaking to (the most common type of adjustment)
- *divergence* - speakers make their speech dissimilar from the speech of the addressee

People use convergence to show solidarity and similarity with the person they are speaking to (which is based on a universal desire for approval). Divergence is much less common - an example would be an English middle-class Oxford graduate emphasising his Oxford accent when communicating with a speaker from a lower socio-economic status.

The factors which influence convergence or divergence are all about identity. People adjust their speech either because the participants in the conversation regard themselves as members of the same group, or one participant would *like* to be regarded as a member of the social group of the second participant, or perhaps the two participants represent groups which are in conflict.

Dominant and subordinate language groups

In multilingual communities one language group is usually politically and economically the dominant one, and there are one or more subordinate language groups. The dominant language may be the *lingua franca* (language of business and trade), may even be an 'official' language of the country, or is the one that 'educated people' speak. So, in terms of linguistic behavior, the most typical pattern of speech adjustment is convergence from the minority language group to the dominant language group. For example, a Papua New Guinean who probably speaks three or four languages will use the most flawless English he is capable of with foreign English speakers, even if they both speak Tok Pisin (a PNG trade language) well. This is not surprising given that there are often real advantages in terms of power and/or living standards if people acquire a high level of competence in a second, more dominant language, one that is used in higher education, government offices and in business.

Many of those involved in minority language development projects - developing alphabets and written materials, in translation work or literacy program development - find that their first task is to motivate and encourage minority language speakers to value their language, and that it is a positive thing for them to have books in their language, and for them to learn to read and use their own language in new ways and for different reasons.

It is not always the case that a minority language is undervalued. Language is sometimes used as a powerful force to assert nationalism, such as with the Basque minority which strongly encourages all its members to learn and use the ethnic language of the Basque community to raise nationalistic self-awareness.

Language and National Identity

A number of prominent historians, sociologists, and political scientists have argued that the existence of a national language is the primary foundation upon which a national identity is built. But national identity is complex, because of the politics involved.

LANGUAGE AND IDENTITY

To take the example of the British Isles - for centuries their linguistic pattern was a patchwork of local dialects, Germanic or Celtic in origin. Only in modern times did individuals motivated by nationalistic ambitions of various kinds set about to establish 'languages' for the nations of England, Ireland, Scotland, and Wales, as well as for Cornwall and other smaller regions (which often constitute 'nations' in the eyes of their more fervent partisans). In the case of Scotland, two separate national languages emerged (Gaelic and Scots), and partisans of the two languages have focused much of their energies on combating the rival claims of the other, rather than arguing against the wide use of English. The vast majority of Scots consider the strategic economic value of using a world language (English) as greatly outweighing the political, cultural, and sentimental value of the 'heritage' languages. The struggle between Gaelic and Scots continues, but English is the accepted dominant language.

Language and Ethnic Identity

Ethnic identity is sometimes used as a synonym of national identity, but it is helpful to make a distinction:

- *Ethnic* identity is focused more on common descent (common ancestors and a common history) and on a cultural heritage shared because of common descent rather than on political factors (like borders, currencies, governments, etc.).
- *National* identity is focused on political borders and autonomy from other nations.

There are many people groups in the world today who share an *ethnic* identity - but who geographically live across the borders of different nations. This situation is quite common in the world today, but particularly in Asia and Africa. In South East Asia, many groups who are part of one ethnic people group live in several different nations. Many of these people may also speak the dominant language of the nations in which they live, but their *primary* identity would be with their people group in which they share a heart language and cultural heritage.

The chart below describes the distribution of the people who would identify themselves as "Lahu" people - who all speak the Lahu language but live in five different nations just in South East Asia. The Lahu girls pictured live in the USA.

By Country	Population	Primary Language
China	516,000	Lahu
Laos	2,900	Lahu
Myanmar	147,000	Lahu
Thailand	34,000	Lahu
Vietnam	7,800	Lahu

Many ethnic people groups are even more widely distributed, such as the HmongNjua:

By Country	Population	Primary Language
China	51,000	HmongNjua
France	124,000	HmongNjua
French Guiana	3,400	HmongNjua
Laos	196,000	HmongNjua
Suriname	2,000	HmongNjua
Thailand	43,000	HmongNjua
United States	107,000	HmongNjua
Vietnam	Unknown	HmongNjua

Language and Religious Identity

Language (or a part of a language, such as an alphabet) can also be a marker or symbol of religious identity. (When we refer to *Christianity* in the paragraph below, it is as an official religion, not necessarily the true Church).

Christian Europe used Latin, the Islamic world uses Arabic, and the Jewish people use Hebrew, all because of their religious identity. When Christianity underwent an East-West split, the use of Latin (as opposed to Greek) became its most potent symbol. The groups of Christians within the western Asian lands ruled by Muslims identified themselves by the languages of Syriac, Chaldean, and other languages.

Jewish communities living in Europe used Hebrew loan words, which distinguished their speech from that of other German and Spanish speakers. Religious splits in Islam came to be associated with dialectal differences in Arabic. Language was often thought of, or used, to reinforce the difference between one religious group and another. Members of the various religious groups needed and wanted to be able to recognise one another, and to identify members of other groups. Language was, and continues to be, an important part of religious identity.

Alphabets and official languages

Language is such an important part of identity, that even the alphabet people use can become a controversial and divisive issue. This is because the preference of one alphabet over another is often tied to a religious or social identity or a tradition. Countries who choose the Arabic alphabet often do so because it expresses an ideology -

"It is natural that the alphabet in which the Qur'an was written should become an integral part of a vision of the world: an external manifestation of belonging to the Ummah, the Islamic community. Countries opting for it would thereby declare their Islamic identity, and its use would amount, accordingly, to a form of confession of faith." (Hegyi)

In China, where unity is a key issue in such a large and diverse country, the Chinese script has been seen for generations as a unifying force. This same script is used for many separate spoken languages or dialects.

"Orthographic battles are common in situations 'where identity and nationhood are under negotiation'; this is because 'orthographic systems cannot be conceptualised simply as reducing speech to writing but rather ... are symbols that carry historical, cultural, and politicised meanings." (Woolard and Schieffelin 1994:64)

There are many other examples that illustrate the fact that language and identity are inseparable - too many to cover in this tutorial. For example, in quite a few places, the language used for street signs has been the cause for conflict or even violence. Many countries have officially recognised languages, or language laws relating to the language of education and government, but these decisions are not easy to make. Among the other language speakers of India, the decision to choose Hindi as the official language was seen as an attempt to erase their cultures, and today there are 18 official Indian languages - but the controversy continues today because some languages have a higher status or profile than others.

? DISCUSSION POINTS

1. Does your language or dialect affect your identity? In what ways?

2. Do you identify others in your community by the way they speak? How?

➡ ACTIVITIES

1. Choose one of the languages other than English that is spoken in Australia.

Research the linguistic community you chose - where are they located in Australia, do they have community groups, cultural activities, or is there any indication you can find that they identify (within the broader Australian society) with their separate cultural identity? Find out where else in the world that language is spoken and how many speakers there are. Try to find a member of that community and talk to them about language and identity issues.

5.19 Languages and Dialects

OBJECTIVES OF THIS TUTORIAL

This tutorial looks at the issues surrounding the definition of a dialect - what is the difference between a language and a dialect, and how are languages separated?

How many languages are there?

The usual number given is up to about 7,000 languages spoken in the world today. But it is difficult to be certain exactly how many languages there are for a few reasons: we still don't know enough about the linguistic situation in some areas of the world, and it can be difficult to distinguish separate languages from dialects of a single language.

Language and dialect

So what is the difference between a language and a dialect? The term 'dialect' is often misused to mean a non-standard variety of a language, or for indigenous languages spoken by small numbers of people (many of these are actually separate languages).

The technical, linguistic definition of the distinction between 'language' and 'dialect' involves the principle of *mutual intelligibility*.

- If two groups of people speak differently from one another, but can still understand one another, then they are speaking different dialects of one language.
- If two groups of people speak differently from one another, and they cannot understand one another, then they are speaking different languages.

Dialects are different, but *mutually intelligible varieties of a language*.

For example, if someone who speaks Australian English meets someone from the USA, they will notice that they speak differently – have different pronunciations, use some different words, maybe even some different grammatical structures, but they can still understand each other. So American English and Australian English are different dialects of one language.

But if someone who speaks Australian English meets someone from Germany, they will

LANGUAGES AND DIALECTS

not be able to understand one another (unless the Australian has learnt German or the German has learnt English). So German and Australian English are separate languages, even though they are very closely related.

The Difficulty with Dialects

This definition of a dialect seems quite simple, but it is a bit more complicated than that... because there is an exception to the general rule:

- If two groups don't understand one another, but there's an unbroken chain of people between them who *do* understand one another, then they are said (by linguists) to be speaking dialects in a continuum that belongs to a single language.

For example, if someone from Sydney meets someone from Glasgow speaking Scottish English, and someone from New Orleans speaking Louisiana English, they would have a lot of difficulty understanding one another. Does this mean that Australian, Scottish and Louisiana English are distinct languages? No, because each of these speech varieties are connected by a chain of speakers who can understand one another: e.g. speakers in northern England understand Scottish speakers, speakers in southern England understand speakers in northern England, speakers in Australia understand speakers in southern England. This is called a *dialect continuum*.

There are several dialect continuums in Europe. We usually think there are many languages in Europe - French, Italian, Spanish, Portuguese, etc. This is because each of these is associated with a different country, and each country has its own 'standard'

Romance languages are in green. Western Romance doesn't include Romanian.

language. But most of the languages of Europe actually belong to just a few dialect continuums. The languages we just mentioned - French, Italian, Spanish and Portuguese - belong to a dialect continuum we call *Western Romance*. It is a continuum because there is no point between Sicily at the bottom of Italy and Lisbon in Portugal where people in one region can't understand people in the neighbouring region, even across national boundaries like the boundary between France and Italy – there is no point where the chain of mutually intelligible dialects is broken.

This makes it hard to come up with the exact number of languages there are in the world. Should we count Portuguese, Spanish, French and Italian as separate, even though they belong to the Western Romance dialect continuum? If we do, then we are counting different dialects in the same dialect continuum as separate languages, just because they are considered standard languages.

But for most dialect continuums in the world, such as in Africa or in Papua New Guinea, there is no dialect that is considered to be a standard dialect. This means we'd be counting European languages differently (by counting more of them) than those in other parts of the world. If we do count Spanish, French, etc. as separate languages, should we also count Catalan (spoken in southern Spain around Barcelona) and Provençal (spoken in southern France), which are as different as Standard Spanish and Standard French?

Another problem is that in many parts of the world we only know about some of the languages or dialects in a region, but we don't know much about many of the dialects in between – so they could be separate languages, or they could also be linked by a chain of mutually intelligible dialects.

Another issue is when social, cultural or political criteria clash with linguistic criteria. Sometimes one language is treated as several languages by its speakers or their governments. Sometimes when a people group crosses borders, the single language they speak will be called different names in each country. For example, Danish and Swedish are the same language, but the people of Sweden call the language they speak Swedish, and the people of Denmark call the language they speak Danish, and these are the official names of the national languages of these countries.

In other cases several languages are treated as one language. Mandarin, Cantonese, Hakka and Hokkien are all officially treated as dialects of one language - 'Chinese' - even though they are not mutually intelligible. So should these all be counted as one language? In Fiji there are two indigenous languages (each separate dialect continuums) - Western Fijian and Eastern Fijian - but all are usually referred to by their speakers and by the government as dialects of 'Fijian'.

Problems with mutual intelligibility

Another reason it is difficult to accurately count the world's languages is because there are some complications with the idea of mutual intelligibility. One problem is that dialects that are part of the same continuum may have unequal relationships to one another.

For example, Australians are used to hearing a lot of American English through movies and television, but most Americans have seen few, if any, Australian movies or television, or met Australians, so they are not used to hearing Australian English. Australians are more likely to understand Americans, but those same Americans might not understand them.

Another problem is that it is difficult to get a true understanding of how much mutual intelligibility there actually is, because there are often identity issues involved when people are asked if they understand or speak another language. For example, where there is a dominant language, speakers of the dominant group might *say* they do not understand the speech of members of the non-dominant group.

In many places in Africa there may be several languages and dialects spoken in an area, but one will be more dominant than the others. Often speakers of the subordinate languages will say they understand the more dominant one, but speakers of the dominant language will not admit to understanding any of the others. This situation follows directly from issues such as the economic and political dominance of the speakers of the dominant language. These attitudes are not unusual, which makes testing mutual intelligibility very difficult.

The same pattern is found within the Scandinavian dialect continuum. Danes claim to be able to understand Norwegians, much better than Norwegians claim to be able to understand Danes.

Languages and speakers

So, we have established that it is difficult to be accurate when counting the world's languages - but we do know that there are approximately 7,000 truly separate languages in the world.

These are not distributed evenly, either geographically, or in numbers of speakers. Some regions have a very high concentration of languages (e.g. West Africa, Indonesia, Papua New Guinea, Amazonia and the Caucuses). Others have a low number of languages (areas of low density are often areas where colonisation has taken place and a dominant language has become firmly established, while others have been lost).

If languages were distributed evenly, each language would have about 1 million speakers - but that is not the reality at all. The number of speakers of languages varies very widely. A few languages have a great number of speakers - 389 languages (6%) have more than 1 million speakers. 94% of the world population speak only 6% of world languages.

Just 6% of the world population speak 94% of languages.

Approximate numbers for the 10 languages with over 100 million speakers:

(numbers are in millions)	as first language	as second language
Mandarin	1,000	180
English	350	850
Spanish	350	60
Hindi/Urdu	250	165
Arabic	225	245
Portuguese	220	20
Bengali	200	40
Russian	165	110
Japanese	130	1
German	100	60
Total	2,990	1,731

This chart simplifies what is a very complex picture - as each of these languages is actually a network of dialects. As we know, English is a large, complex dialect network.

Arabic is a dialect continuum. Like Western Romance in Europe, it has some country-specific standard varieties. Speakers of Moroccan Arabic at one end of the continuum and speakers of Iraqi Arabic at the other end would not be able to understand

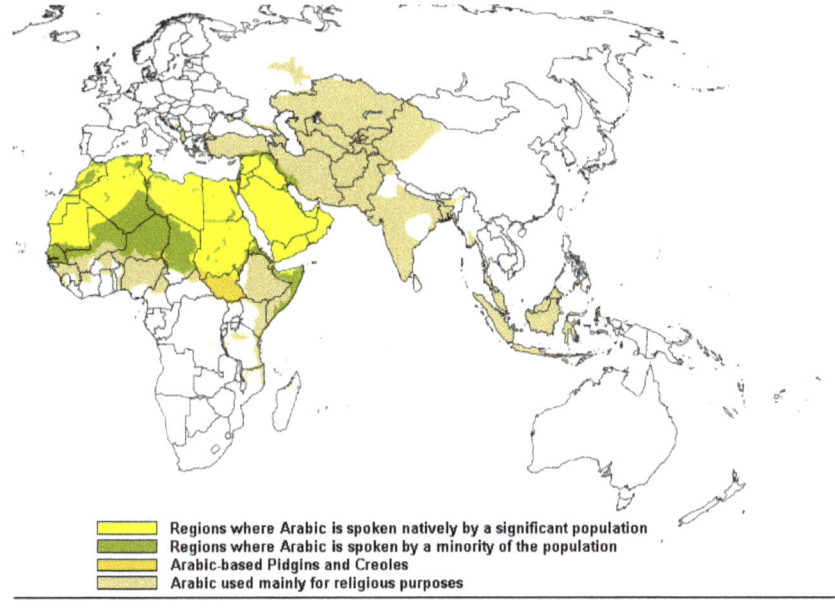

Regions where Arabic is spoken natively by a significant population
Regions where Arabic is spoken by a minority of the population
Arabic-based Pidgins and Creoles
Arabic used mainly for religious purposes

LANGUAGES AND DIALECTS

each other, but there is no point between Morocco and Iraq where a chain of mutually intelligible dialects is broken. (Many Arabic speakers also speak Classical Arabic, which links them.) If we count Arabic as one language and add up all its speakers, then to be consistent we should do the same with the European dialect continuums. We should really count Western Romance as one language with 715 million first language speakers.

The language with the greatest number of speakers, referred to as 'Mandarin', consists of a huge number of dialects, many of which are not mutually intelligible. There are eight main Mandarin dialect areas in mainland China (in bold below), and each of these areas contains other related dialects:

Beijing mandarin: Beijing dialect, Standard Mandarin, Chengde dialect, Chifeng dialect, Hailar dialect, Karamay dialect

Ji Lu Mandarin: Baoding dialect, Jinan dialect, Shijiazhuang dialect, Tianjin dialect

Jianghuai Mandarin: Hefei dialect, Hainan Junjiahua, Nanjing dialect, Nantong dialect, Xiaogan dialect, Yangzhou dialect, Jiao Liao Mandarin, Dalian dialect, Qingdao dialect, Weihai dialect, Yantai dialect

Lan Yin Mandarin: Dungan language, Lanzhou dialect, Urumqi dialect of Chinese,

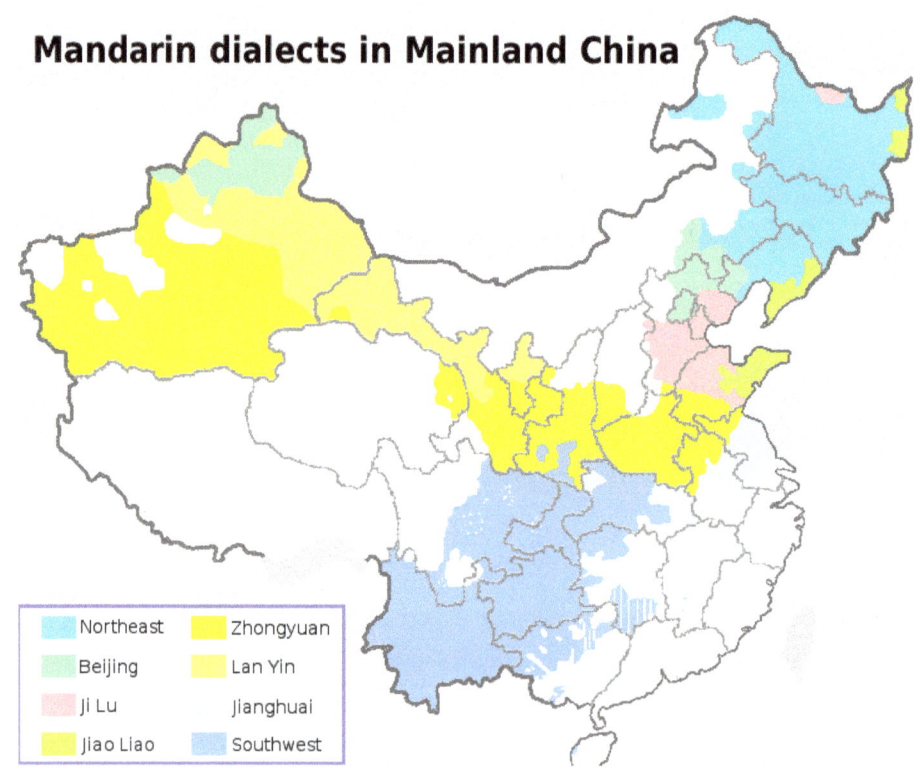

Xining dialect, Yinchuan dialect

North-east China Mandarin: Changchun dialect, Harbin dialect, Qiqihar dialect, Shenyang dialect

South-western Mandarin: Changde dialect, Chengdu dialect, Chongqing dialect, Dali dialect, Guiyang dialect, Kunming dialect, Liuzhou dialect, Wuhan dialect, Xichang dialect, Yichang dialect

Zhongyuan Mandarin: Hanzhong dialect, Kaifeng dialect, Kashgar dialect of Chinese, Luoyang dialect, Nanyang dialect, Qufu dialect, Tianshui dialect, Xi'an dialect, Xuzhou dialect, Yan'an dialect, Zhengzhou dialect

In contrast to Mandarin and the other very large languages mentioned above, most languages in the world have only a few thousand or even a few hundred speakers. Many have just a handful of very elderly speakers, like the Aboriginal language Gajirrabeng which is now spoken only by one old lady living in Western Australia (at left).

Estimates predict that between 50% and 90% of all languages in the world will die out within this century. It is estimated that on average, every two weeks, a language somewhere in the world falls into disuse.

DISCUSSION POINTS

1. What do you think about language death? What is being lost? Should we set out to preserve languages? How does it relate to communicating Truth?

LANGUAGES AND DIALECTS

➡ ACTIVITIES

1. The tutorial mentioned that Australian and American English are different dialects of English. Write down some examples of different pronunciations, words or grammatical structures in a comparison table. (You could use another dialect of English you are more familiar with for your comparison.)

2. Find a website that has a map of the world's endangered languages. Choose one of these languages and try to research some more information about it (e.g. Why is it endangered, what languages are replacing it, is anything being done to preserve it? etc.)

3. Below are some words used in British or American English for which a different word is used in Australian English. Try to identify if the word is British or American and then give the Australian equivalent.

- faucet
- dungarees
- cookie
- push-chair
- aubergine
- monkey wrench
- fall (season)
- bobby
- pacifier
- drugstore
- diaper
- anorak
- electric fire
- sophomore

✓ ANSWERS

Word	British or American?	Australian Equivalent
faucet	American English	tap
dungarees	British English	jeans
cookie	American English	biscuit, bikkie
push-chair	British English	pram, stroller
aubergine	British English	eggplant
monkey wrench	American English	adjustable spanner, pipe wrench
fall (season)	American English	autumn
bobby	British English	policeman
pacifier	American English	dummy
drugstore	American English	chemist
diaper	American English	nappy
anorak	British English (from Eskimo: *anoraq*)	warm jacket/coat parka (from Aleut via Russian)
electric fire	British English	(electric) heater
sophomore	American English	year 10 high school student

5.20 Language Families

> **OBJECTIVES OF THIS TUTORIAL**
>
> This tutorial looks at the various ways that separate languages might be connected to one another, and why some languages are said to be members of the same language family.

Introduction

There are a variety of ways that languages can be connected to one another. One important way is by being members of the same *language family*.

Change is a natural process in language, and all languages are always changing. No matter how old you are, during your lifetime you have probably noticed new words and phrases being introduced, or existing ones changing their meaning, or and some falling out of use all together. Over time, because of things like geographical, cultural or religious factors, a language can change differently in different places, and diverge into separate dialects, then eventually into separate languages. Those separate languages are related to each other in a single language family. We say they are in the same family if they come from the same original source language. For example, the Romance languages are all derived from Latin. This is a linguistic result of the wide influence of the Roman Empire.

Often there is no direct information about the ancestor language because most ancient languages were never written down. But the family relationship between languages can be established by identifying relationships between their words and sounds. Linguists can then reconstruct aspects of the common ancestral languages that they came from.

There are written records of Latin, the ancestor of the Romance languages, so the family relationship is easy to establish, but there are no written records of the ancestors of the Germanic or Celtic languages. Linguists have worked to analyze these languages and have established that they are in fact descendants of an original Germanic language and Celtic language.

LANGUAGE FAMILIES

Language families

Today several hundred unrelated language families in the world have been recognized, but the exact relationships between languages and subgroups are regularly questioned and reassessed.

Most of the world's languages can be grouped into 40 or 50 major language families. These 'major' families are ones that have a large number of languages and/or a large number of speakers. There are only a few dozen languages that are 'isolates' - languages that can't be shown to be related to any other language, e.g. Basque (South-western France and North-eastern Spain).

The top four major language families are:

- *Indo-European* - which has well over 2 billion speakers
- *Sino-Tibetan* - with well over 1 billion speakers
- *Niger-Congo* - which has half a billion speakers
- *Afro-Asiatic* - with a quarter of a billion speakers

Indo-European

The Indo-European language family is very large, and includes most of the languages of Europe, but it also extends beyond Europe.

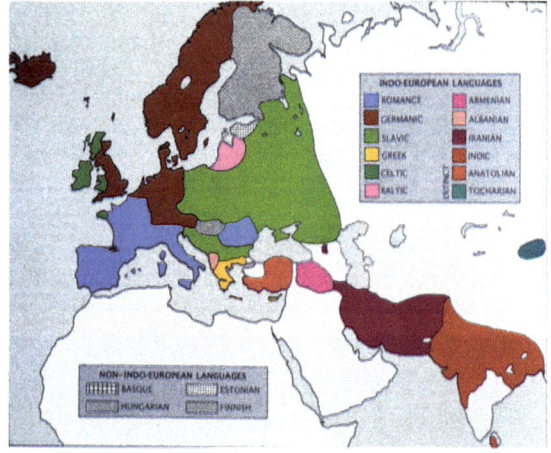

Many of the languages of western Asia (like Persian in Iran, Pashto in Afghanistan, and Kurdish) and of the northern half of the Indian subcontinent (such as Hindi/Urdu, Punjabi and Bengali) are Indo-European languages.

European colonial expansion in the last few centuries has also taken Indo-European languages around the world, and in many regions outside Europe they are spoken as the first language by most of the population, like in North and South America and Australia.

Language families in the region of Australia

The three main linguistic groupings in this region are Australian (i.e. Aboriginal languages), Austronesian, and Papuan. The region has some of the greatest linguistic diversity in the world, containing about 1,600 languages - one quarter of all languages.

Australian

Australian Aboriginal languages belong to a single language family, because research has concluded that they are descended from a common ancestor language. At the time of colonization by Europeans in 1788 there were around 260 Aboriginal languages. Today about 145 are still spoken.

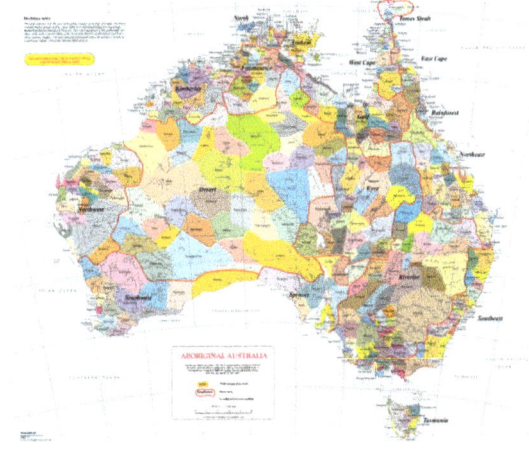

Very few of these remaining languages are spoken by more than a few hundred people, and many by only a handful of elderly people. Half have fewer than 10 speakers. Only 18 Australian languages are being learned by children today, which means that the rest will be extinct when the current generation dies out.

A small handful of Aboriginal languages are spoken by over a thousand people. The largest Aboriginal languages, with more than 2,000 speakers (each with several dialects) are:

- *Western Desert* (Central Australia, 5,800 speakers),
- *Kala Lagaw Ya* (Western Torres Strait islands, 3,000-4,000 speakers),
- *Warlpiri* (Central Australia, 3,000 speakers),
- *Eastern Arrernte* (Central Australia, 2,175 speakers).

The Australian language family has several branches. Across most of Australia the languages belong to one branch, called *Pama-Nyungan*. This includes all of Australia except the Top End (the far north of the Northern Territory and Western Australia) and is shown in yellow on the map at right.

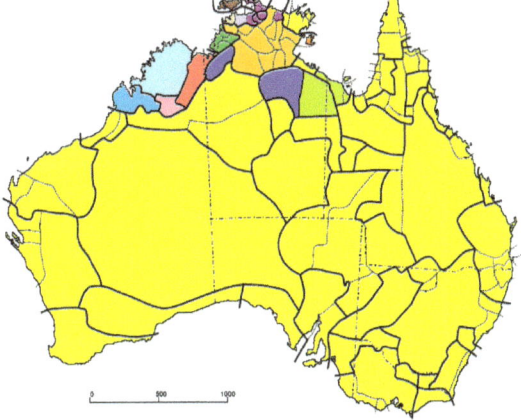

The other languages belong to about a dozen branches that get grouped together as *Non-Pama-Nyungan*, but these branches are not more closely related to each other. So, there are about a dozen branches of the language family 'Australia', of which Pama-Nyungan is one.

In Tasmania the indigenous language-speaking population was destroyed so quickly that very little is known about the

LANGUAGE FAMILIES

languages there. It is thought that there were between 8 and 12 languages spoken in Tasmania. But so little is know about these languages, that it is not clear how they were related to each other, and there is no evidence that they were related to the mainland languages. Because there is no evidence that they are not related to other Australian languages, they are assumed to be members of the Australian family.

Austronesian

A very large and important language family in the region of Australia is *Austronesian*. These languages all belong to a single family, and are descended from a common ancestor language. Today there are more than 1,200 Austronesian languages spoken, with about 300 million speakers.

Austronesian languages are the indigenous languages of:

- Taiwan (not of the current Sinitic-speaking Chinese majority)
- The Philippines
- A few coastal points on mainland South East Asia (mainly Vietnam)
- Malaysia
- Indonesia
- Many coastal areas of the island of New Guinea
- Much of island Papua New Guinea
- Melanesia (Bougainville, Solomon Islands, Vanuatu, New Caledonia and Fiji)
- Polynesia (including New Zealand, Samoa, Tonga, Hawai'i, Easter Island)
- Micronesia
- Madagascar

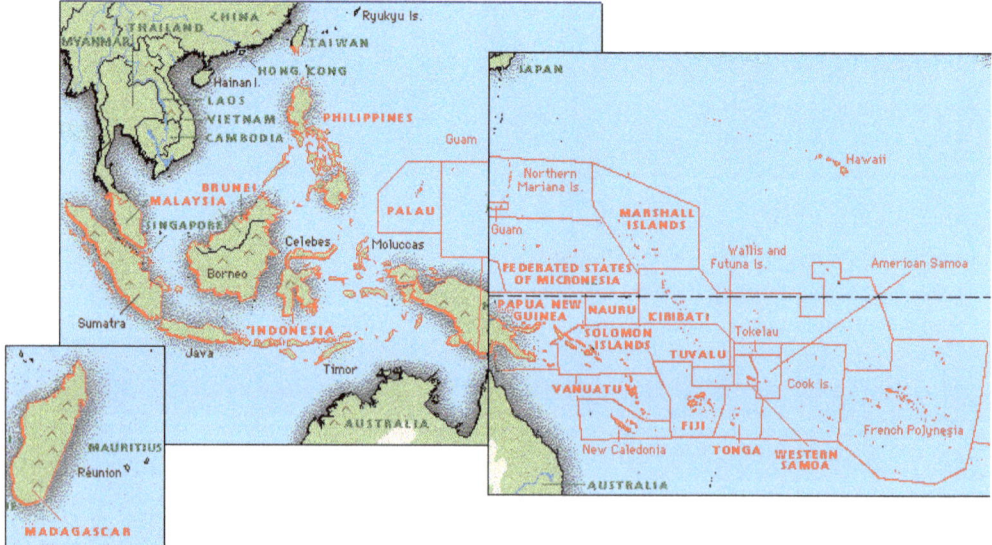

Almost all speakers of Austronesian languages speak various languages of the western Austronesian branches - mainly in Indonesia, Malaysia and the Philippines. Many languages of Indonesia and the Philippines have several million speakers - Javanese has about 75 million speakers.

But there are many Austronesian languages with only a few thousand or even a few hundred speakers. The Oceanic branch of Austronesian (Papua New Guinea, Melanesia, Polynesia and most of Micronesia) has hundreds of languages but includes less than 2 million speakers in total. For example Vanuatu has about 105 languages with a total population of about 150,000 speakers.

Papuan

The term Papuan refers to a group of languages that are in the same region and of the same type - but it is made up of at least 60 separate language families. There are more than 750 Papuan languages in the group.

Papuan languages are spoken on:

- the island of New Guinea (comprising the nation of Papua New Guinea, plus the Indonesian province of West Papua);
- parts of some of Papua New Guinea's offshore islands;
- parts of some islands of eastern Indonesia (including in parts of Timor);
- some parts of the Solomon Islands.

About 5 million people speak a Papuan language, but most are spoken by only a few hundred people, or a few thousand at the most. Only three are spoken by more than 100,000 people. The largest Papuan family is *Trans-New-Guinea*, found across most of mainland New Guinea. It has about 500 languages, including several large languages like Engan and Chimbu. Another large family is *Sepik-Ramu*, with about 100 languages, all spoken by small numbers of people. Another large Papuan family is *Torricelli*, with about 50 languages, also spoken by small numbers of people.

Some other major language families

Uralic

Hungarian is not an Indo-European language, but belongs to the Ugric branch of the Uralic family. Finnish, Estonian, and some smaller European languages belong to the Finnic branch which is also of the Uralic family. Most Uralic languages are spoken further east in Siberia.

LANGUAGE FAMILIES

Altaic
Turkish is the most westerly member of the Turkic branch of the Altaic family, that also includes other languages of Central Asia like Azerbaijani and Uzbek, and some as far east as western China, such as Uighur. Other branches of Altaic include Mongolian.

Dravidian
The languages of southern India belong to the Dravidian family, including Tamil, Telugu and Malayalam.

Sino-Tibetan
The Sino-Tibetan family has two main branches. *Sinitic* contains the main languages of China, such as Mandarin, Cantonese and Hakka. *Tibeto-Burman* contains languages such as Tibetan, Burmese and Karen.

Other languages of East Asia
Japanese and Korean are not definitely known to be related to each other or any other language, but many people think they are distantly related to Altaic. Ainu is the indigenous pre-Japanese language of the Japanese islands. It is an isolate.

Niger-Congo
This is the largest language family of Africa. Most people in Sub-Saharan Africa speak a Niger-Congo language. The biggest and most important branch is *Bantu*, with languages such as Swahili, Zulu, Rwanda and Xhosa. Other branches include languages like Igbo, Yoruba and Fulani in Nigeria, and Akan in Ghana.

Afro-Asiatic
This family is found throughout North Africa, North-east Africa and the Middle East. One important branch is *Semitic*, which contains Arabic, Hebrew, Maltese and Aramaic. Other branches include languages such as Berber, Hausa, Somali, Coptic and Ancient Egyptian.

Other families of Africa
The *Nilo-Saharan* family is located in east central Africa and contains languages such as Nubian. The *Khoisan* family is located in south-west Africa and includes the so-called 'click languages'.

South-east Asia

There are quite a few language families in South-east Asia. One is *Austro-Asiatic*, including languages such as Vietnamese and Khmer (Cambodian). Another is *Tai-Kadai*, including languages such as Thai and Laotian.

The Americas

North, Central and South America contain many indigenous language families. Some families in North and Central America include:

> **Eskimo-Aleut**, with languages in the Arctic (including in north-east Asia) such as Greenland Inuit and Yupik.
>
> **Algonquin**, with languages such as Blackfoot, Cheyenne and Cree.
>
> **Na-Dene** with languages such as Navajo and Apache.
>
> **Hokan-Siouan** with languages such as Mohawk and Sioux.
>
> **Aztec-Tanoan** with languages such as Comanche and Nahuatl.
>
> **Mayan** with languages such as Tzeltal and Quichean.

There are many language families in South America, and not much is known about some of them. Some of the better known families include:

> **Quechuan**, with descendants of the languages of the Incas such as Quechua.
>
> **Carib**, with the indigenous languages of the Caribbean.

Language Families of the World

- Indo-European
    - Albanian
    - Armenian
    - Baltic
    - Celtic
    - Germanic
    - Greek
    - Indic
    - Iranian
    - Romance
    - Slavic
- Sino-Tibetan
    - Chinese
    - Tibeto-Burman
- Afro-Asiatic
    - Berber
    - Chadic
    - Cushitic
    - Semitic
- Altaic
    - Mongolian
    - Tungusic
    - Turkic

- American Indian (several families)
- Australian (several families)
- Austro-Asiatic
- Austronesian
- Basque
- Caucasian
- Dravidian
- Eskimo-Aleut
- Japanese (possibly Altaic)
- Khoisan
- Korean (possibly Altaic)
- Niger-Congo
- Nilo-Saharan
- Paleo-Siberian (several families)
- Papuan (several families)
- Tai-Kadai
- Uralic

Relationships between languages

Languages that belong to the same language family often have similarities in their grammar, which makes sense because they have inherited a lot of their grammar from their original ancestor language.

But languages that are not of the same family can also resemble each other for other reasons. Languages in the same geographical area can resemble each other even though they may not be members of the same language family. This happens because languages that are in contact with each other can influence each other over time.

For example in some coastal regions of Vietnam, some small Austronesian languages (belonging to the Chamic subgroup of Austronesian) are interspersed among Vietnamese, which is an unrelated Austro-Asiatic language. Many speakers of Chamic languages are bilingual with Vietnamese. Most Chamic languages have many grammatical characteristics that look more like Vietnamese than their Austronesian relatives elsewhere.

On the island of Bougainville, communities living side by side speak languages belonging to the Austronesian and two separate Papuan families, and many people are bilingual. Many Papuan languages have the word order Subject + Object + Verb (SOV). Most Austronesian languages are either VSO or SVO, but some Austronesian languages have the same order - SOV - as their Papuan neighbors. Some Bantu languages are spoken in areas of southern Africa close to where the Khoisan languages are spoken and they have developed clicks.

Similarities like these are due to mutual borrowing and influence and do not necessarily indicate that the languages are in the same family. This kind of influence of one language on another can lead to *convergence* of languages in a particular area. One example of convergence is the Balkans - Greek, Bulgarian, Albanian and Serbo-Croat are only distantly related, but share many features. Also in central India, where there are two completely separate language families (Indo-European and Dravidian), the languages

ACTIVITIES

share many features in common.

1. Find out more about one of the indigenous Australian languages that are still spoken today. How many speakers does it have, is the language written, is it taught to children, what written materials are available, are the speakers multi-lingual and in what other languages?

2. Determining if languages are related can be difficult - apparent similarities could be the result of common origins or might just be because of language contact. One way to see if languages are truly related is to look at basic vocabulary such as terms for body parts, close kinship terms, common features of the natural world (e.g. river, sun, cloud) and words for the low numbers. These words are usually resistant to being 'borrowed' from other languages and so similarities in these words would show that languages are related. Consider the following data from five European languages. Which do you think are related and why? Try to work it out before looking at the answer and explanation below.

Finnish	Hungarian	Basque	Estonian	Spanish	*gloss* (definition)
kala	hal	arrain	kala	pez	*fish*
lintu	madár	xori	lind	ave	*bird*
sarvi	szarv	adar	sarv	cuerno	*horn*
pea	fej	buru	pää	cabeza	*head*
silmä	szem	begi	silm	ojo	*eye*
käsi	kéz	esku	käsi	mano	*hand*
jalka	láb	oin	jalg	pie	*foot*
tähti	csillag	izar	täht	estrella	*star*
pilvi	felhő	hodei	pilv	nube	*cloud*
puu	fa	zuhaitz	puu	árbol	*tree*

LANGUAGE FAMILIES

✓ ANSWER

vihreä	zöld	berde	roheline	verde	*green*
kaksi	kettő	bi	kaks	dos	*two*

Finnish and Estonian are the most closely related, and both are more distantly related to Hungarian. Basque and Spanish are not related to any of the other languages - the similarity in the words for 'green' is due to a case of borrowing. To support the conclusion that Finnish and Estonian are related we can point to a number of words that are identical in both languages (*kala, puu*), or that vary just in the final sound (*sarvi-sarv, kaksi-kaks*). There is a consistent pattern that word-final *-i* in Finnish has been lost in Estonian, as well as a less-consistent loss of word-final *-u* and *-a*. These two Finno-Ugric languages are also related to Hungarian, but more distantly. We can see a consistent *p* → *f* sound shift between Finnish and Hungarian, and also word-initial *s* → *sz*. *k* and *l* in the Finnish data is often retained in the Hungarian, but can be inconsistent.

5.21 Language Change

OBJECTIVES OF THIS TUTORIAL

All languages are in a constant state of change. This tutorial looks at how languages change over time and why the changes occur.

Introduction

All living languages are constantly in a gradual process of change. No doubt you have noticed this about your own language and can probably think of a few words that you once used, but would no longer say today. But it isn't just words that change in languages - change can affect many areas of language, such as:

- Semantic change (meaning change)
- Syntactic change (sentence structure change)
- Morphological change (change in the function of the smallest units of meaning)
- Phonological change (sound change)

We will be looking at each of these areas of change in more detail in this tutorial.

Why is it important to understand how languages change? Because understanding the ways languages change helps to give us a clearer understanding of how a region may have developed and how the people groups in an area may share a common history and therefore cultural similarities. In a geographical region where there are a number of related languages, it probably means that they once spoke a single language that has changed and diverged over time into separate languages and dialects.

Looking at the mechanics of language change can help us to answer questions like: What has changed? How did it change? Why did it change? How can we find out what earlier forms of a language were like? Also, for those involved in language development projects - translation, literacy development, or curriculum development - it is important to consider the fact that every language is in a process of change. As we develop materials in a language, we are not looking for some "pure form" of the language, but the most widely communicative form of the language at the time.

LANGUAGE CHANGE

Semantic change

Words can change meaning over time, and there are several different kinds of meaning change that are common. Word meanings can change in how wide the meaning is. For example, meanings can become narrower, like these words in English:

Old English		Modern English
deor 'animal'	→	*deer* 'a kind of animal'
mete 'food'	→	*meat* 'flesh food'
hund 'dog'	→	*hound* 'hunting dog'
fugol 'bird	→	*fowl* 'domesticated bird'

The meanings of words can also become broader over time, for example:

Old English		Modern English
bridde 'baby bird in nest'	→	*bird* 'bird'
dogge 'a breed of dog'	→	*dog* 'dog'

Note the interesting switch with dog and hound – *dog* used to mean a particular kind of dog, while *hound* meant any kind of dog. Now they have changed meanings, as have *bird* and *fowl*.

Words can also change their meaning to a related but different meaning. We call this a *semantic shift*. For example:

[Middle English] *bede* 'prayer' → [Modern English] *bead*
[Old English] *bux* 'a kind of tree' → [Modern English] *box*

This kind of meaning change happens when a word develops a broader or additional meaning, then the original meaning disappears. About one hundred years ago *gay* only meant 'happy' or 'fun'. Then it developed the additional meaning of 'homosexual' as well as the original meaning of 'happy'. Then people gradually stopped using it to mean 'happy', and now it is only used to mean 'homosexual'.

Words mostly change meaning gradually, so there is a chain of small meaning shifts, often over a long period of time. These small shifts can add up to some major changes in meaning over time. The English word *black*, for instance, originally meant 'white', and is related to words like *blank*, *bleach* and *bald*. The original word, *bhleg* comes from the original Indo-European language, and meant 'white'. Then in the original Germanic language it changed to *blakaz* - 'to blaze'. This then changed to mean 'to have blazed', then 'to be burned', then 'black'.

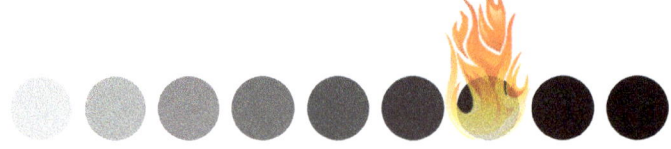

Meaning change can also involve words changing to have a more positive meaning than they originally had. For example:

Old or Middle English		Modern English
cniht 'boy, youth'	→	*knight* 'high ranking armoured man'
nice 'stupid'	→	*nice* 'pleasant'
prætig 'tricky, sly'	→	*pretty* 'attractive'

Words that have changed to have a more positive meaning more recently:

terrific 'terrifying'	→	*terrific* 'very good'
wicked 'evil'	→	*wicked* 'very good'

Words can also change to have a more negative meaning:

Old or Middle English		Modern English
sely 'blessed'	→	*silly* 'foolish'
gebur 'farmer'	→	*boor* 'boring person or thing'

Semantic change can also come about when the word for a part of something is used to refer to the whole thing - for example, saying *wheels* for 'car', or using *tongue* to mean 'language'.

Another reason meanings can change is because of word avoidance or word taboo. A community can decide they don't want to say a particular word, so they use another word as a replacement to mean the same thing. The new meaning of the replacement word becomes its standard meaning.

For example, the original Indo-European word for 'bear' was *rtko*. In northern Europe bears were common and very dangerous, and people were scared to even say the word for them, so in early Germanic the word was avoided and people referred instead to *beron* 'the brown one'. This word came down to Old English as *bera*, then to modern English as *bear*. It also came down to Swedish as *björn*, and German as *Bär*.

Syntactic change

Grammatical structures can also change over time. Even basic word order involving subject, object and verb can shift. In Old English the basic word order was SOV (Subject Object Verb).

    Hēo   hine   lærde.
    'she   him   advised'
      S   O   V

LANGUAGE CHANGE

In Modern English the basic word order is SVO.

She advised him.
 S   V   O

Sometimes the grammatical structure can change to make the sentence simpler:

I am going to go. → I'm gonna go.
I have got to go. → I've gotta go.

The argument structure of a language can also change. For example, in Middle English verbs to do with mental activities needed subjects in accusative case. Now they need subjects in nominative case:

Me likes it. → I like it.
Me thinks... → I think...

Morphological change

Remember that morphemes are the smallest units of meaning in a language, which can include things such as affixes and intonation - they are not necessarily words.

One way languages can change on the morphological level is by losing inflections. For example, Old English nouns belonged to one of three different genders or noun classes, and each gender had four case forms for each noun. So for the noun *hund* 'hound', there were six different forms - *hund, hunde, hundes, hundas, hundum, hunda* - depending on the gender (masculine, feminine or neuter) and case (nominative, accusative, dative or genitive). In Modern English all genders have disappeared and all case endings have disappeared except genitive (possessive), so we only have *hound*, *hound's* and *hounds'*.

The opposite also happens, when morphemes join together to become a single morpheme -

going to → gonna
got to   → gotta
ought to → oughta
have to   → hafta

Another type of morphological change is *reanalysis* - when speakers re-analyse part of a word as if it was a morpheme, when originally it had not been a separate morpheme in that word.

For example, *hamburg-er* was originally a 'kind of food from Hamburg'. Then various other forms such as *beefburger, cheeseburger, vegeburger*, etc. were used. This created a new morpheme - *burger*.

208

Another example of reanalysis is the word 'mugaccino' - meaning a mug of cappuccino coffee. The noun *cappuccino* originated in the 1940s from the Italian, and means coffee made with milk that has been frothed up with pressurised steam. It comes from the Italian word 'Capuchin,' because its color resembles that of a Capuchin's habit (a friar belonging to a branch of the Franciscan order). Speakers treated the word as if it was spelled *cupaccino*, with the first part being the morpheme *cup*. Then it was simply a matter of changing this morpheme to *mug*. Other recent new forms that use the new morpheme *-ccino* are *mochaccino* and *chococcino*. *Frappuccino* (trademarked by Starbucks in the 1990s) uses the word *frappé* (Greek 'iced coffee') with the morpheme *-ccino*.

Phonological change

The most important kind of change in language for understanding the way languages are related to each other is phonological (sound) change. Sound changes tend to apply consistently throughout a language, so they let us see sound correspondences between related languages. That helps us see how languages within a family group together into branches, or subgroups. There are many kinds of sound changes. We'll look at a few of the most important ones:

Lenition

Languages change to become more efficient. One way this happens is that sounds that take more effort to produce, change to sounds that require less effort. This is called *lenition*, or weakening. Voiceless sounds require more effort than voiced sounds, so one common form of lenition is for voiceless sounds to become voiced over time.

Also, the more that the mouth is closed when producing a consonant, the more effort is needed. The various manners of articulation can be listed from strong to weak (those that take more effort are first): stops, fricatives, nasals, laterals, approximants. The Uradhi language (Aboriginal, northern Queensland) shows lenition: [p] (a voiceless stop) in the ancestral language has changed to [w] (a voiced approximant) in the modern language.

pinta	→	winta 'arm'
pilu	→	wilu 'hip'
pata	→	wata 'bite'

The fullest form of lenition is for a sound to weaken so much it disappears completely.

LANGUAGE CHANGE

In the Kara language (Austronesian, New Ireland, PNG), all vowels at the end of a word have disappeared. Also, the [p] (a voiceless stop) has changed to [f] (a voiceless fricative):

  tapine → tafin 'woman'
  punti → fut 'banana'
  topu → tuf 'sugarcane'

In Standard Fijian (Austronesian, Fiji), it is the final consonants that have been lost:

  tangis → tangi 'cry'
  ikan → ika 'fish'
  bulan → vula 'moon'

Another form of weakening is when a cluster of consonants are simplified by one of the consonants disappearing. In English, word-final clusters like [mb] and [ŋg] were reduced by losing the final stop:

  læmb 'lamb' → læm
  hæŋg 'hang' → hæŋ

Assimilation

Another very common kind of change occurs when a sound is affected by the other sounds around it. Sounds can become more like the sounds around them. This is called assimilation.

Complete assimilation involves a sound becoming exactly the same as a sound next to it.

  <u>Original Germanic</u>   <u>Icelandic</u>
  findan → finna
  gulð → gull
  unðan → unna

In partial assimilation, sounds change to become more like the sounds next to them in some way. One common kind of assimilation is *palatalisation*, where a consonant changes its place of articulation to become palatal when it's next to a front vowel. For example, in English [k] changed to [tʃ] before front vowels (like [i] and [e]).

  <u>Old English</u>   <u>Modern English</u>
  [kinn] → [tʃɪn] 'chin'
  [kɛsi] → [tʃiz] 'cheese'
  [kirike] → [tʃɜtʃ] 'church'

TUTORIAL 5.21

? DISCUSSION POINTS

1. How does your language differ from your grandparents' language? Try to think of specific instances of language change that has taken place in the time since they were young.

2. What are some of the influences that have brought about these changes?

➡ ACTIVITIES

1. Do some further reading on the history and development of Australian English.

2. Search online for the words coffin, caravan, giant, and humor (use this American English spelling), to see where they originally came from and how they have changed in meaning and usage over the years. How do you think Australian English might change over the next ten years, and why?

3. Below are two Middle English recipes with Modern English spelling below. Consider each one and note the words you have never heard before, or any words that seem to be used differently to their modern sense.

Connynges in Cyrip (Rabbit served in a wine-currant sauce)

Take connynges and seeþ hem wel in good broth. Take wyne greke and do þerto with a porcioun of vynegar and flour of canel, hoole clowes, quybibes hoole, and ooþer gode spices, with raisouns coraunce and gyngyuer ypared and ymynced. Take vp the connynges and smyte hem on pecys and cast hem in to the siryppe, and seeþ hem a litel in fere, and serue it forth.

Modern English Spelling: Take conies and boil them well in good broth. Take Greek wine and do there-to with a portion of vinegar and flour of cinnamon, whole cloves, cubebs whole, and other good spices, with currants and ginger pared and minced. Take up the conies and cut them in pieces and cast them into the syrup, and boil them a little in the fire, and serve it forth.

Caudell (A frothy wine or ale-based drink)

Take faire tryed yolkes of eyren, and cast in a potte; and take good ale, or elles good wyn, a quantite, and sette it ouer þe fire / And whan hit is at boyling, take it fro the fire, and caste þere-to saffron, salt, Sugur; and ceson hit vppe, and serue hit forth hote.

Modern English Spelling: Take fair tried yolks of eggs, and cast in a pot; and take good ale, or else good wine, a quantity, and set it over the fire / And when it is boiling, take it from the fire, and cast there-to saffron, salt, Sugar; and season it up, and serve it forth hot.

(Recipes from: http://www.godecookery.com)

5.22 Language Types and Variation

OBJECTIVES OF THIS TUTORIAL

This tutorial looks at how different languages can be said to be the same *type* of language because of specific features they share. It will also look at language variation, and why there can be different varieties of the same language.

Language Types

We saw that languages can be related to each other because they belong to the same language family. We also saw that unrelated languages can be similar because they have been in contact with each other. But there is a third kind of relationship languages can have with each other – they can be related in *typology*.

Geographically widely separated languages that are not part of the same language family may still share features. This is due to the fact that there are universal tendencies for languages to have certain combinations of characteristics. For example, there are languages all around the world that have the basic order Verb + Object + Subject (VOS), but this tells us nothing about whether they are in the same language family or geographically close to one another, they simply share that feature.

Just because two languages have similarities does not mean they are related. Many Papuan languages share the clause order Subject + Object + Verb (SOV) with languages of India such as Hindi. Many Austronesian languages share the clause order Subject + Verb + Object (SVO) with English. We will look at some examples of different languages and the major features that unrelated languages can share. These features can be phonological, morphological or are related to the syntax.

Phonology

One difference in the phonology of languages is that some languages use tone and others don't. This means a group of phonemes together might mean one thing if it is said with rising pitch, and something completely different if said with falling pitch, or with level pitch, etc. In tonal languages, the pitch is just as important a part of the meaning of a word as its phonetic sounds.

LANGUAGE TYPES AND VARIATION

Sinitic languages like Mandarin have tone, and some unrelated South-east Asian languages like Vietnamese and Thai also have tone. Tone is an areal (geographical) feature for South-east Asian languages. But there are many other languages around the world that are not in the same family or geographically related to Sinitic languages that also have tone. For example, *Yoruba*, a Niger-Congo language of Nigeria, *Gadsup*, a Trans-New Guinea language of Papua New Guinea, and *Koasati*, a Hokan-Siouan language of the USA, all have tone. This map shows the distribution of tonal languages in the world -

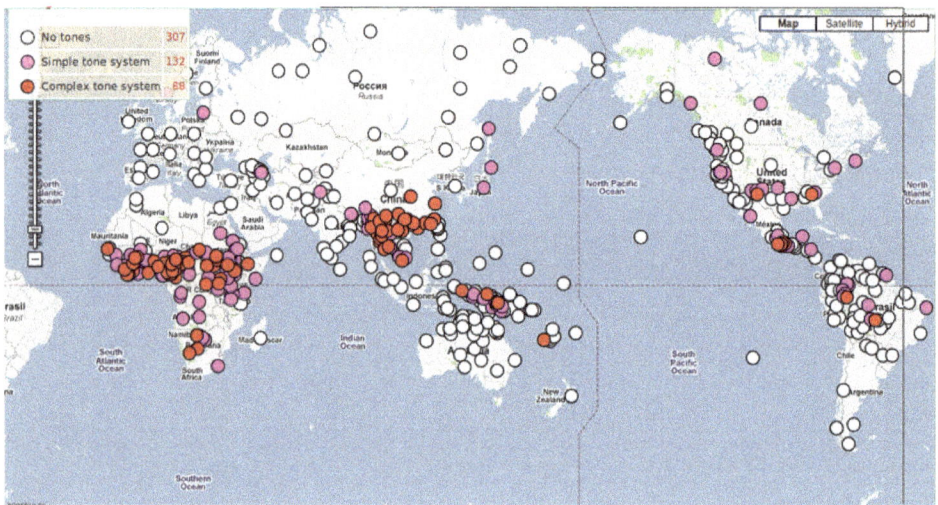

Read more - *World Atlas of Language Structures*: http://wals.info/chapter/13

Morphology

Languages differ in how complex they are in their morphology. There are four types: isolating, agglutinating, fusional and polysynthetic.

Isolating - Mandarin and Vietnamese are examples of isolating languages.

    (1 word = 1 morpheme).
    An example in Mandarin:
    Wǒ gāng yào gěi nǐ nà yì bēi chá.
     I just want for you bring one cup tea
    'I am just about to bring you a cup of tea.'

Agglutinating - Yanyuwa and Finnish are agglutinating languages.

    (1 word = many morphemes; 1 morpheme = 1 function)
    An example from Yanyuwa (Australian Aboriginal):
    Kan-alu-arlkarlba-nthaninya.
    us-they-wash-past.customary
    'They used to wash us.'

Fusional (sometimes called *inflecting*) - Latin and Russian are fusional languages.
>(1 word = many morphemes; 1 morpheme = many functions)
>An example from Latin:
>Regin-a   serv-um   vid-et.
>queen-FEM.SG.NOM slave-MASC.SG.ACC see-3SGSUBJ.PAST
>'The queen saw the slave.'

Polysynthetic - Tiwi and West Greenlandic are polysynthetic languages.
>(1 word = very many morphemes; 1 morpheme = 1 or more functions)
>An example from Tiwi (Australian Aboriginal):
>A-wunu-wati-yi-ma-jingi-kili-ja.
>he-towards-morning-start-with-in-vehicle-go
>'He is coming along in a vehicle in the morning.'

Syntax

Word order in sentences

Languages can be of the same type because they share the same word order. These are all of the possible basic word orders: SVO VOS OVS SOV VSO OSV. Look at the following examples of different languages which all have different word orders:

>English (Subject + Verb + Object):
>>Tom ate the chicken.
>>S   V   O

>Turkish (Subject + Object + Verb):
>>Hasan küz-ü aldi.
>>Hasan ox bought
>>   S   O V
>>'Hasan bought the ox.'

>Fijian (Verb + Object + Subject):
>>E ā raici na koli na yalewa.
>>see the dog the woman
>>   V   O   S
>>'The woman saw the dog.'

>Kokota (Austronesian, Solomon Islands) (Verb + Subject + Object):
>>Ne kati-ni ia mheke ia zora.
>>bite the dog the pig
>>   V   S   O
>>'The dog bit the pig.'

LANGUAGE TYPES AND VARIATION

Hixkaryana (Cariban, Brazil) (Object + Verb + Subject):
Toto ya-hos-ye kamara.
man grabbed jaguar
  O   V   S
'The jaguar grabbed the man.'

Tobati (Austronesian, West Papua) (Object + Subject + Verb):
Honyo foro rom-i.
dog pig see
  O   S   V
'The pig saw the dog.'

Both Verb-Object and Object-Verb languages can be found on every continent and in a number of different language families. If you look at the map below, you will see that in this relatively restricted area - western sub-Saharan Africa - languages of both types are found.

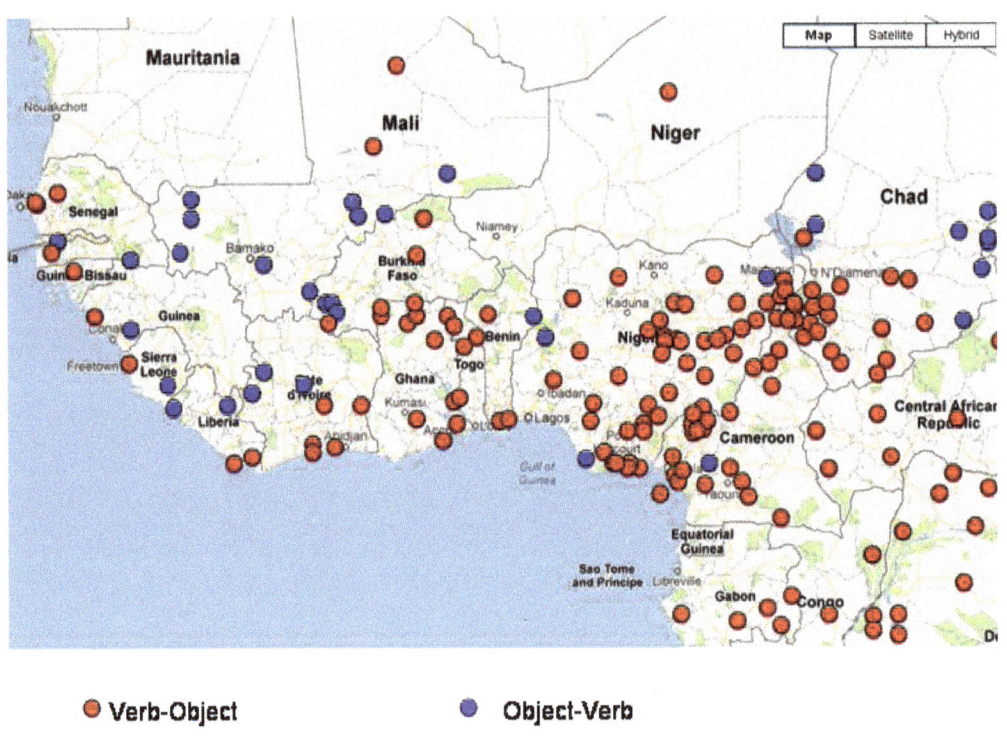

Read more in the *World Atlas of Language Structures Online*

Left-headed versus right-headed

Some languages place the head of a phrase *before* everything else (at the left edge of the phrase). Others place the head of a phrase *after* everything else (at the right edge).

Japanese is a right-headed language. This means that heads come after their dependents: postpositions come after their noun phrase, nouns come after their adjectives and after their possessors, and verbs come after their objects. The heads are in bold below:

Tokyo **ni**
Tokyo [locative]
  NP   P
'in Tokyo'

ookii **kodomo**
 big   child
ADJ   N
'big child'

Taroo   no   **atama**
Taroo [genitive] head
POSSESSOR   N
'Taroo's head'

tori o **tabe-ta**
bird eat-PAST
OBJ V
'ate the bird'

The Malagasy language (Austronesian, Madagascar) is left-headed. This means that heads come before their dependents: prepositions come before their noun phrase, nouns come before their adjectives and before their possessors, and verbs come before their objects. Heads are in bold below:

alim   tana
inside ground
   P   NP
'in the ground'

ny **kiraro** maloto
the shoes dirty
      N   ADJ
'the dirty shoes'

tongotry Rakoto
   foot   Rakoto
    N   POSSESSOR
'Rakoto's foot'

nividy   ny mofo
PAST. buy the bread
        V   OBJ
'bought the bread'

Variation in Language

We have looked at how different languages can share similar features and so be of the same type. Now we are going to look at why one single language can develop different variations. Variation is a central fact of human language – language is never exactly the same as it was before. Even if you recorded yourself saying the same word over and over again and tried to say it exactly the same way, there would still be slight variations each time.

Most variations in pronunciation aren't significant because the brain doesn't recognise them. As long as the pronunciation of a certain sound is within a certain range, it doesn't matter a lot how the sound is produced – the brain will recognise all examples from within the acceptable range as being a particular sound. However, if you intend to make sound A but you actually

make a sound within the pronunciation range for sound B, then the brain will notice that there has been a variation.

This is actually what does happen in language over time. So, for example, the sounds [aɪ] and [ɔɪ] are very similar to one another. You can think of them as adjacent units on the continuum of sound. Most of the time, variations in the pronunciation of [aɪ] go unnoticed. But, sometimes, people cross the boundary between the two, and this is noticeable. People do notice when a word like *my* is pronounced as [mɔɪ], or indeed *like* is pronounced as [lɔɪk].

Over long periods of time, these kinds of changes accumulate and you can get great differences. About 2,000 years ago English and German were one single language, but over time, with the accumulation of various changes, they have become quite different from one another. This same kind of gradual change has happened all over the world. But change doesn't have to produce different languages – it can also produce different *varieties* within a language. There are two main kinds of variation – geographical and social.

Geographical variation is described in terms of the concepts *dialect* and *language*. We looked at what a dialect is in a previous tutorial, but we will do a quick review:

Dialect: Two speech varieties are regarded as dialects of a single language if they are mutually intelligible.

Language: Two speech varieties are regarded as different languages if they aren't mutually intelligible.

Remember that there is an exception to this rule? Two speech varieties which aren't mutually intelligible can still be dialects of an overall language. If there is a chain of mutually intelligible varieties, then they are analysed as dialects of an overall language.

Geographical (Dialect) differences in Australian English

Geographical variation is not a very noticeable feature of Australian English. This is probably because of the high rates of mobility of the Australian population since the beginning of settlement. Other areas with high population mobility since the beginning of colonisation, like western Canada and the western United States also show no immediately noticeable regional variation.

But, even though it isn't very noticeable, there is a regional variation in Australian English. Some people have identified different dialects of Australian English - they are consistently different but mutually intelligible. The table below shows the percentage of people who use a 'short A' rather than a 'long A' sound in the words at the left. You can see that speakers from South Australia have significantly lower frequencies of short A than speakers from elsewhere. Similar patterns are found for other pronunciations and show regional variations.

	Brisbane	Melbourne	Sydney	Hobart	Mt Gambier	Adelaide
dance	100	95	93	89	89	73
advance	94	90	86	86	4	18
plant	97	92	82	82	4	0
grasp	0	3	30	15	2	9
giraffe	0	0	4	19	0	0
mask	3	0	0	0	0	0

Social (Dialect) differences in Australian English

People's social background affects which linguistic variety they use when they speak. Every speaker has an accent when they speak, which is associated with their geographical location, and the dialect they speak will have differences in grammar and vocabulary. Some dialects are prestigious when used in some social situations or in some social groups. Historically the most prestigious dialect of English is the Received Pronunciation (RP - the 'Queen's English', or 'BBC English').

It is difficult to separate regional and social factors, because people from a certain region or area are often associated with a certain social class as well. But, it is accepted that in Australia, there are three general dialects or accents of English, *Broad*, *General* and *Cultivated*. These are associated with regional areas and also with social status or class. Even though Australians like to think of themselves as egalitarian and not having social classes, there are expectations that someone with a high socio-economic position will speak a higher-prestige variety of Australian English. The table below shows some of the differences in vowel pronunciation between RP, and the Australian English dialects.

Lexical Sets	RP	Broad Aus E	General Aus E	Cultivated Aus E
BATH	ɑː	aː	aː	aː
NURSE	ɜː	ɜː	ɜː	ɜː
FLEECE	iː	əːɪ	+i	ii
PALM	aː	aː	aː	aː
FACE	eɪ	ʌːɪ, aːɪ	ʌɪ	ɛɪ
GOAT	əʊ	ʌːʊ, aːʉ	ʌʉ	Öʊ
GOOSE	uː	əːʉ	ʊʉ	ʊu
PRICE	aɪ	ɒːɪ	ɒɪ	aɪ
MOUTH	aʊ	ɛːo	æo	aʊ
NEAR	ɪə	ɪə, iːə, iː	ɪə, iːə, iː	ɪə
SQUARE	ɛə	eə	eə	eə
START	ɑː	aː	aː	aː
CURE	ʊə	ʊə, ɔː, uːə, uː	ʊə, ɔː, uːə, uː	ʊə, ɔː, uːə, uː

ACTIVITIES

1. If you haven't done so already, search online to read and research further on variations in Australian English. Listen and compare other world dialects of English. YouTube is a good resource for this kind of search.

2. What word would you use for each of the following?
- Processed sausage-like meat often used in sandwiches.
- Small red skinned sausages.
- Cardboard single serve containers of fruit juice.
- Item of clothing worn when swimming.

LANGUAGE TYPES AND VARIATION

✓ ANSWERS

1. This meat is generally known as *devon* in Sydney and on the East coast, *fritz* in South Australia and *polony* in Western Australia. It is also variously known as: *beef Belgium, Belgium sausage, Byron sausage, Empire sausage, fritz, German sausage, luncheon sausage, polony, pork German, Strasburg, wheel meat or Windsor sausage*.

2. Most commonly referred to as *frankfurts* (or sometimes *frankfurters*). Generally a *frankfurt* is a large sized one, rather than the little ones used for party snacks - which are most commonly called *cocktail frankfurts*, *little boys* and *cheerios* (in Queensland).

3. In New South Wales it is referred to as a *popper*, in other states it is usually referred to as a *fruit box* or a *juice box*. A possible reason it is called a popper is, that when a young kid finished with the contents (or even if they were not) they would blow the popper up like a balloon and the stamp on it "popping" the "popper". This would perhaps spray others in juice. Usually after lunch hour there would be flat poppers spread across the schoolyard. Sometimes they are also referred to by popular brand names, such as *Prima*.

4. *Bathers* seems to be the most generic term used. Other terms include: *swimmers, cossie, costume, swimsuit* or *togs*. More specific terms are *bikini, speedos, racers, sluggos,* or *boardies* (*boardshorts*). *Trunks* is sometimes used, but usually by expatriate British.

www.ingramcontent.com/pod-product-compliance
Lightning Source LLC
Chambersburg PA
CBHW061811290426
44110CB00026B/2847